The Old Deeside Road Revisited

An Explanation of What Remains

Best Wishes

Graham J. Marr

Graham J Marr

NORTH-EAST SCOTLAND CLASSICS

DEESIDE BOOKS, BALLATER

2014

Reprinted 2019, 2022

Published by Deeside Books,
18-20 Bridge Street,
Ballater,
Aberdeenshire AB35 5QP
Tel. 01339 754080
Email: deesidebk@aol.com
Web: www.deesidebooks.com

© Graham J Marr 2014

ISBN: 978-1-907813-07-8

NORTH EAST SCOTLAND CLASSICS:

1. Lochnagar by Alex Inkson McConnochie.
2. Loch Kinnord by The Rev. John Grant Michie.
3. Donside by Alex Inkson McConnochie.
4. Aberdeen Street Names by G. M. Fraser.
5. Strathspey by Alex Inkson McConnochie.
6. Ben Muich Dhui and his Neighbours.
   by Alex Inkson McConnochie.
7. The Old Deeside Road Revisited by G. J. Marr.
8. The Mounth Passes by G. J. Marr.
9. The Dee and Don Passes by G. J. Marr.
10. The Scenery of the Dee by Jim Henderson.

HISTORY AND TRADITIONS OF SCOTLAND SERIES:

1. The Tales Behind the Tunes of Glory
   by Stuart Gordon Archer.
2. The Ballater Memorial by John Burrows.

Also distributed by Deeside Books –
Plant & Roots: A Social History of Ballater by Ian Cameron.

Printed and bound by Robertson Printers, Forfar.

Contents

List of Illustrations

My photographs of existing Old Deeside Road sections.

List of Illustrations

Comparison of Fraser's photographs with the current location.

Foreword

The format of this volume of the *North-east Scotland Classics Series* is different to its predecessors in that it is not a straightforward reproduction of a scarce local history book. Rather, this work is more of a complete reassessment of an academic and historical study undertaken almost one hundred years ago. Because this book compares and contrasts with the original it was decided to include it within the series.

The possibility of publishing an update to G. M. Fraser's *The Old Deeside Road* was a project that was enthusiastically agreed to when approached by Graham Marr, and the book has finally come to fruition after a tremendous amount of groundwork over several years by the author. The result is an excellent record of the development of one of the major transport links between Aberdeen and part of its hinterland, and consequently, those parts of the old Deeside road that still remain on the ground since Fraser's time have now been accurately recorded.

It might be opportune here to give a synopsis of G. M. Fraser's life and also a brief description of the original edition of *The Old Deeside Road*. George Milne Fraser was born at Methlick, Aberdeenshire, in 1862 and came from farming stock. He was employed in the granite industry in his youth, but the loss of an eye through an accident caused him to move to a journalistic career. For many years he was a reporter with *The Aberdeen Free Press* and also *The Evening Gazette*. This brought him into contact with many influential people of an academic, political, religious and business nature, and this encouraged him to produce numerous articles on both contemporary events and local history. His knowledge of local affairs was probably one of the reasons that he was successful in his application to become Librarian of Aberdeen Public Library, a position he held from 1899 until his death in 1938. During this period he was still producing articles for the press, but these were also now supplemented by the publication of a number of books on the local area.

Foreword

The majority of his books were concerned with Aberdeen and included such titles as *The Green and its Story* (1904); *Historical Aberdeen* (1905); *Aberdeen Street Names* (1911); *Bridge of Dee* (1913); *The Aberdonians and other Lowland Scots* (1914) and *Historical Walks and Names* (1927). However, his largest and most detailed work was *The Old Deeside Road (Aberdeen to Braemar): Its Course, History and Associations*, first published in 1921. This latter book was published on behalf of the Aberdeen Natural History and Antiquarian Society and was number three in their series. As Fraser notes in his introduction to this volume, it took over five years to complete, and the original hardback edition ran to 276 pages plus 21 pages of illustrations and a large fold out map that was bound in at the rear.

This fold out map was at the relatively small scale of two miles to the inch and consequently it is rather difficult to decipher much of the information contained therein. Also there have been considerable changes to various road alignments over the last one hundred years and it was therefore decided not to include a copy of the original map in this new volume. Instead, it was decided to include a series of smaller scale Ordnance Survey (OS) extracts to use as location maps and then to refer the reader to the specific larger scale 1:50,000 or 1:25,000 OS maps where required. Coordinates of all of the relevant points discussed have been included in the text so that the reader can use this book in conjunction with the OS maps to identify features on the ground. Many parts of the old road still exist and are therefore still identifiable as features on the OS maps and are particularly recognisable on the larger 1:25,000 series.

Fraser uses the terminology "with illustrations from original photography" in the 1921 edition, and where these features still exist this current volume has attempted to recreate a modern comparison from the same viewpoint. In many cases it is surprising how consistent both of these views are, and indeed, how much has still survived. Also, for ease of identification, the current author has included additional photographs within the text to support his findings on the ground, and these are a useful source of corroboration.

It is known that Fraser had a particular interest in the Deeside area and was a founder member of the Deeside Field Club, and took part in many of their excursions and field trips. He was also a regular contributor to the *Deeside Field*, their magazine that was printed every few years after the first volume was published in 1922.

The original edition of *The Old Deeside Road* in its A4 hardback form is now reasonably scarce, although it is still obtainable on the out of print market. However, there were later paperback editions published in the 1980s in the smaller A5 format, and although now long out of print, should still be obtainable at a more modest price. However, by using this current volume in conjunction with the modern OS maps the reader should be able to identify those parts of the old Deeside road that still exist without reference to the previous editions.

It is hoped that this modern work will prove a useful addition to all those that have an interest in the local history of the Deeside area. As always, further information is available on out of print sources, either from the shop or by contacting us via the website.

Bryn Wayte,

Deeside Books,

Ballater.

www.deesidebooks.com

Introduction

At the start of the 21st century the journey from Aberdeen to Braemar is relatively straightforward. From the centre of the city the A93 can be followed along the Dee valley through a variety of towns and villages to Braemar, from where the road continues south by Glen Clunie to Glen Shee and onwards to Perth. It seems a logical route for people travelling on it today, following the River Dee for much of the distance, and passing through the main settlements along the way. However, in reality this road has a relatively short history, and some of the settlements are also comparatively new in the historical context of the Dee valley and its road connections.

If we look back to the early history of movement through the Dee valley the main traffic was based on north to south routes. The passes traversing the spine of hills running from Drumochter in the west to Aberdeen in the east were the principal roads for long distance commerce. This line of high ground is generally known as the Grampians or the Mounth, and the passes are referred to as the Mounth passes. Apart from the most westerly routes which link Speyside to Blair Atholl, these passes linked the Dee valley to the markets of the south for cattle, sheep and whisky and also labour for harvests. But they did not only connect Deeside to the south. The Mounth passes also provided connections with the towns and villages of Aberdeenshire and Moray to the north of the Dee valley. Thus it can be seen that the droving of livestock and other commerce was primarily concerned with linking the northern producers with southern middlemen and consumers. Consequently, in earlier days, the development of an east to west route along the length of the Dee valley was probably limited to local needs. Markets tended to be based on an area about twenty miles around a commercial centre, which in most cases was a village or town. The local roads would have linked farms and estates with the nearest market. Therefore the Deeside road as defined here may well have grown organically by connections between local routes to form a through route along the Dee valley.

It seems likely, as reflected in the current road network, that a road developed along both the north and south sides of the Dee. However, the north side has the main settlements and has probably always been the more important road for the development of Deeside. Essentially the route followed in this book is the north Deeside road, with a link to the south side of the River Dee in the Braemar area.

In the 17th century the Scottish Parliament legislated for powers to levy charges on local landowners to pay for the repair of roads, and for tenants to provide free labour to work on these roads for up to six days a year. The system was not very successful, and informal attempts were made to commute the labour into cash payments in order to employ a more skilled labour force. Roads maintained under this method were called commutation roads. By the end of the 18th century most roads were still in too poor a condition to support the growth of trade, and a law was drafted to make commutation of labour compulsory. However, it was overtaken by a move to create a Turnpike Act in 1795. This put responsibility for roads into the hands of the larger landowners (as turnpike trustees) who decided routes, toll gate sites, and charges for use of the road.

Within ten years the main routes out of Aberdeen were all improved, but the roads tended to carry large debt burdens as tolls were insufficient to pay off construction costs. The development of the railways also adversely affected the turnpike system by diverting toll paying traffic onto the faster rail network. In 1866 the Aberdeenshire Roads Act set up road maintenance as a charge on property rates and the toll gates were removed.

The above developments took place under the control of the civil authorities. In parallel to this, following the 1715 campaign by the Jacobites, new roads were developed by the British military authorities to ensure that control over the Highlands could be maintained. Although the objective was to avoid further rebellions, 1745-46 saw a final unsuccessful attempt to reinstate the Stuart dynasty. On Deeside this military work resulted in a road being built from Braemar to Balmoral, which included the scenic old

Invercauld Bridge. The overall route ran from Coupar Angus to Fort George, a distance of approximately 100 miles, and was built between 1748 and 1757.

The A93 between Aberdeen and Braemar is largely the improved and modernised version of the turnpike road dating from developments starting in 1796. The Deeside turnpike was the first one in Aberdeenshire, running initially from Mannofield in Aberdeen to the Mills of Drum near Crathes. It was subsequently extended along the Dee valley to Braemar. The interesting historical question is whether variations and improvements over the past couple of hundred years have obliterated earlier roads, or were new road lines taken at various times, thereby leaving some traces of the older routes as a glimpse into the past. The objective of this book is to try and identify which of these scenarios might have taken place by examining the evidence on the ground today. Wherever possible this evidence will be supported by the use of old and new plans and maps, photographs, written details and, of course, G. M. Fraser's original book.

While I have been familiar with what is now the A93 from Aberdeen to Braemar for many years, I had not really considered what might have preceded it by way of a road along the north side of the Dee valley. I obtained a copy of G. M. Fraser's *Old Deeside Road* when it was reprinted in 1980. On reading it, I became aware that there was much more to the history of the Deeside road than was immediately obvious on the ground. While some of his writings could be related to the route of the modern A93, some of his descriptions seemed to cover areas away from the present main roads. This set me off on a search to find and photograph anything that might remain of the Old Deeside Road which he described. It was surprising how much could still be found by going out and exploring the areas he covered. I decided to produce some record of the Old Deeside Road as it is, around ninety years after Fraser's investigations. However, the intention is not to rewrite or reproduce Fraser's book, but to provide a guide which can be used in the field to discover the interesting historical byways which once formed the main road communication along the Dee valley. To do this, most of Fraser's original figures have been included and I have produced comparable photographs to illustrate the same locations as they are now. I have included these in the text where they are most relevant to my own journey along the Old Deeside Road. The retention of Fraser's figure numbers has meant that some of them appear out of sequence from his original, and I hope it does not detract from the interest in them. I have also included a number of additional photographs that I feel show the most interesting aspects of the Old Deeside Road along the way. The old road is divided into what I hope are logical chapters, linking the main communities on the route, under the following headings:

Aberdeen to Peterculter; Peterculter to Banchory; Banchory to Aboyne; Aboyne to Ballater; The Ballater Area; Ballater to Braemar; The South Deeside Road; The Braemar Area; Intersection with the Mounth Passes.

Maps and Further Information

Maps

A vital resource for any investigation of the Old Deeside Road on the ground is the use of maps which cover the route. G. M. Fraser included a map in his book in which he categorised the sections of the old road. Different markings were used depending on whether the Old Deeside Road was still in use in various forms, or had been obliterated altogether. It can be difficult to follow the route on his original map because of its small scale of two miles to one inch, and it has not been reproduced in this book. Maps are included in this book which show the Old Deeside Road sections still visible on the ground, but at a fairly general level of detail.

The best maps to use for finding the route on the ground with a practical level of detail are the Ordnance Survey 1:25,000 Explorer series (listed below).

It is worth noting that I have adopted place name spellings from the current Ordnance Survey maps. There are undoubtedly local and historic place names which vary from these, but for the ease of readers finding the old road locations on maps I have decided to use the Ordnance Survey versions.

The Ordnance Survey **1:50,000 Landranger Series** is probably the best known set of maps, and can be used as follows to cover the length of the Old Deeside Road:

Sheet 38 Aberdeen covers Aberdeen City to Bridge of Canny area.

Sheet 37 Strathdon & Alford covers Bridge of Canny area to Crathie.

Sheet 44 Ballater & Glen Clova covers Kincardine O'Neil to west of Inver.

Sheet 36 Grantown & Aviemore covers Crathie to Inver but omits the section just west of Inver.

Sheet 43 Braemar & Blair Atholl covers the Invercauld to Braemar area along with Glen Clunie.

The Ordnance Survey **1:25,000 Explorer Series** is at a larger scale with additional detail, and the following maps cover the route:

Sheet 406 Aberdeen & Banchory covers Aberdeen City to west of Bridge of Canny.

Sheet 395 Glen Esk & Glen Tanar covers from west of Bridge of Canny to Cambus o' May.

Sheet 388 Lochnagar, Glen Muick & Glen Clova covers Cambus o' May to Invercauld.

Sheet 387 Glen Shee & Braemar covers Braemar and Glen Clunie, but Braemar is at the top of the map and some of the route is off this sheet.

Sheet 404 Braemar, Tomintoul & Glen Avon covers Crathie to Braemar.

Map References

In the text I have included grid references to assist in finding locations on maps or on the ground using GPS or similar systems. For readers not familiar with the UK Ordnance Survey grid referencing system I have copied the following explanation from their blog which I hope will be of assistance.

http://www.ordnancesurvey.co.uk/blog/2013/03/map-reading-skills-learn-how-to-use-grid-references/

The National Grid

Before we look at what the grid reference numbers mean, it's important to understand the wider picture of the National Grid. Ordnance Survey divides Great Britain into 100 km by 100 km squares, each with a two-letter code. The two-letter codes can be found printed in faint-blue capitals on Ordnance Survey maps and can also be found in the map key.

The first letter, for example 'S', denotes 500 km by 500 km squares and this is subdivided into 25 squares that are 100 km by 100 km within it, making 'ST', 'SU', 'SO' and so on. There are four main first letters: 'S', 'T', 'N' and 'H' covering Great Britain, plus an 'O' square covering a tiny part of North Yorkshire that is usually below tide. A unique National Grid reference should have this two-letter descriptor followed by the grid reference numbers within that square.

National Grid Reference Numbers

The numbers going across the map from left to right are called eastings, and go up in value eastwards, and the numbers going up the map from bottom to top are called northings, because they go up in a northward direction.

There are two main types of grid reference:

- four-figure grid reference, such as '19 45', indicates a 1 km by 1 km square on the map; and
- six-figure grid reference, such as '192 454', indicates a 100m by 100m square on the map.

Sometimes you may also come across:

- eight-figure grid reference, such as '1926 4548', indicates a 10m by 10m square on the map; and
- ten-figure grid reference, such as '19267 45487', indicates a 1m by 1m square on the map

In practice, it's the six-digit grid reference number that is most commonly used, although the more digits used gives you a more precise location. GPS devices often specify at least eight-digit grid reference numbers.

Six-figure Map References

In the example below, the shaded box is in the four-figure grid reference square '18 44', but more accurately it is 7 tenths across and 8 tenths up within that larger grid square, therefore the six-figure map reference is '187 448'.

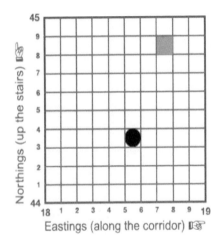

The shapes on the diagram above have the following six-figure grid references:

Shaded square – 187 448
Circular dot – 185 443

To avoid confusion about which part of the National Grid you are referring to when you quote the six-figure grid reference you should put the two letters of the area you are in before the numbers. For example, you may be at grid reference '509 582' in south-west Scotland. The complete grid reference you should quote would be 'NX 509 582' (without the letters the numeric reference would be repeated in every 100 km square).

(End of Ordnance Survey blog extract, Ordnance Survey © Crown copyright 2014)

Historical Maps

A number of historical maps show features of interest with regard to the Old Deeside Road. The maps discussed here are available at the National Library of Scotland, and can be viewed on their website www.nls.uk within their Digital Resources section.

A map by Alexander Milne of 1789 is interesting in that it shows how the Hardgate and the Deeside Road left the centre of Aberdeen. As the Hardgate heads south, the junction where the "Road from Brae Marr to Aberdeen" diverges to the west is clearly shown. The Hardgate is titled "Bridge of Dee Road" from this point onwards.

That map pre-dates the development of Union Street and Holburn Street which subsequently made major changes to the city street pattern. John Wood's map of Aberdeen from 1828 has these new streets, and clearly shows the line of the new Holburn Street separating the Hardgate from the Old Deeside Road. The latter is shown as only a double dotted line for a short distance. The reason for this is that a new "Deeside Road" has appeared taking the route which would become Great Western Road, and latterly the A93 to Braemar. This emphasises the fact that Great Western Road, and its continuation the A93, is a more modern route to Deeside, and is not the Old Deeside Road, which became, and still is, Broomhill Road.

A map related to the Great Reform Act of 1832 reflects the fact that by this time the Deeside turnpike would have been developing into the main route to Deeside. This map shows the two Deeside roads when they were presumably both in use at the same time.

By 1888, when Andrew Gibb & Co. produced a Plan of the City of Aberdeen, Great Western Road is beginning to appear as a main road with building development along it. This probably reflects its use by this time as the main North Deeside Road. The Old Deeside Road, by comparison, looks like a minor road with little development, and is named Broomhill Road with no mention of its former role. It is easy to see on any current street map of Aberdeen.

The Bartholomew map of Aberdeen from 1912 has the road layout much as it is today, with the exception that Great Southern Road had not yet been built. This cuts off from Holburn Street where the former junction of the Hardgate and Old Deeside Road once was, and heads south to the King George VI Bridge over the Dee. Broomhill Road is shown as a city street, but Great Western Road now has the name Deeside Road attached to it beyond Mannofield. By this time it seems likely that the Old Deeside Road had become a byway. Sometime after this G. M. Fraser must have begun his search to find what was left of the road.

The following documents are of interest with regard to the Dee valley in general.

General Roy's military map of 1747-52 shows numerous sections of the road along the north bank of the Dee, which appear to coincide well with Fraser's Old Deeside Road.

However, some sections appear to differ. For example, Roy's map shows the road going to the north of Crathes Castle rather than the southern route by Milton of Crathes. Also, on Roy's map, the road runs to the north of Fraser's Old Deeside Road from Bridge of Canny until it passes the house of Gateside just before Kincardine O'Neil.

It may be that there are older parts of the Deeside road than Fraser's documented route, or one might wonder whether there could be less accurate aspects of Roy's survey.

One map which is of particular interest is the Taylor and Skinner Survey of 1776. This map appears to have been one of Fraser's main sources for the route of the Old Deeside Road, and much of their mapped route is a good match with Fraser's old road sections.

There are other maps available on the National Library of Scotland website which cover the Dee valley, some from the 17th and 18th centuries and also the later Ordnance Survey maps dating from the 19th century onwards. Note that the Ordnance Survey maps all date from after the development of the Deeside turnpike, and therefore the main road shown will be that one, now the A93.

One factor to bear in mind is that the A93 is usually termed the North Deeside Road. However, when it reaches Invercauld it crosses to the south bank for the final few miles into Braemar. Where I have categorised sections of the older roads as north or south, this refers to the bank of the river on which that section lies. References to the south Deeside road between Invercauld and Braemar are to the remaining sections of old, disused roads. What is currently termed the South Deeside Road only runs between Aberdeen at the Old Bridge of Dee and Balmoral Bridge at Crathie. Beyond that it was removed from the public road network because it went through the Balmoral Estate. Its continuation at the west end of Balmoral Estate was replaced by the main turnpike from the Victorian Invercauld Bridge to Braemar.

Further Information

While Fraser's book also covered other aspects such as bridges, ferries and fords on the River Dee, I have for this book concentrated on the old public road along Deeside. A fuller set of photos of what remains of the old road can be found in my Flickr account located at www.flickr.com/photos/grahamstravels in the *Old Deeside Road Album*.

With regard to the old Mounth passes, I have included information on where they intersect the old road. I walked these passes over the years prior to investigating the Old Deeside Road and many of my photographs can be found and browsed in my Flickr account in the *Mounth Passes Collection* located at www.flickr.com/photos/grahamstravels.

Some details can also be found on the useful *Scotways Heritage Paths* website www.heritagepaths.co.uk which includes sections of the Old Deeside Road as well as Mounth passes. This website contains details of many other historic paths throughout Scotland with information on their history and accessibility.

A further source of information on the Mounth passes between Aberdeen and Braemar is contained in the e-book *The Mounth Passes: A Heritage Guide to the Old Ways Through the Grampian Mountains*, which includes a number of my photographs. This is available through Amazon or Barnes and Noble e-books.

Another book which provides descriptions and the social history of many of the Mounth passes is *Grampian Ways* by the late Robert Smith. In addition, Fraser's *Old Deeside Road* also includes two chapters on the Mounth passes which provide valuable background information.

One of the main uses of the Mounth passes was for the droving of livestock, particularly cattle, from the Highlands and North-east of Scotland to markets, eventually providing supplies to consumers in the south. These markets, or trysts as they were known, were held in many places, such as Paldy's Fair at Laurencekirk. The largest of the trysts were held at Crieff, and later at Falkirk, where in the middle of the 19th century almost 150,000 cattle as well as sheep were traded. A great deal of information on droving is contained in A. R. B. Haldane's book *The Drove Roads of Scotland*, and explains why the north to south routes had such importance in the past.

G. M. Fraser wrote another book which is useful in the context of the Old Deeside Road. That book is *Aberdeen Street Names*, in which he provides the history and meaning of many of the older city streets.

Fenton Wyness is included as a source of information through his book *Royal Valley: The Story of The Aberdeenshire Dee*. He also produced *City by the Grey North Sea: Aberdeen*, which provides a history of the city. He includes in it a map showing the street development of the 18th and 19th centuries superimposed on the older road pattern, particularly showing the Hardgate and Union Street in the context of routes to the south.

Turnpike Toll Houses

The Deeside toll houses are an interesting feature. They were built to provide the means of collecting tolls when the turnpike roads were developed. Although they are not strictly related to the Old Deeside Road, because it pre-dates the turnpike development, Fraser lists the Deeside turnpike toll houses in his Appendix C. He points out that there was no complete list of Aberdeenshire toll houses that he knew of. The toll houses were positioned by the roadside so that the toll keeper could watch the road and charge travellers for their usage of the road. The first phase of the Deeside turnpike had toll houses at Cuparstone, in what is now Great Western Road in Aberdeen; also a toll house at Peterculter and one at Mills of Drum. All have now disappeared. Further up Deeside the turnpike had toll houses which Fraser listed at Invercannie, west of Banchory; Kincardine O'Neil, on the main street; toll houses at the east and west ends of Aboyne; Tomnakeist, east of Ballater; Coilacriech, west of Ballater; Inver and Braemar. Of these only three now appear to remain. At Kincardine O'Neil the toll house sits by the A93 near the western end of the village. It is of the usual earlier type, with a semi-circular end onto the road provided with windows to watch the turnpike traffic. The ones at Inver and Braemar are of a later design, when it must have appeared that the turnpikes were being overtaken by railways, and were likely to change to a more general taxation basis for maintenance. These latter houses are more conventional cottages, but still with windows in each gable end to watch the road. It would make them easier to use as houses in the post toll era. The Braemar toll house is illustrated in a later chapter. Inver toll house is at the east end of the group of houses there, near the path to Cairn na Quheen and the nearby section of Old Deeside Road.

Chapter 1

Aberdeen City to Peterculter

Map 1 from Aberdeen City to Cults and Map 2 from Cults to Drumoak cover this section of the old road.

Leaving the city centre for Deeside by Union Street, Holburn Street and Great Western Road, the modern A93 road follows the route developed after 1800 when Union Street was built. This was a time of major expansion of the city, which for centuries had its historic centre around the Green, the River Dee estuary and St Nicholas Church. New developments expanded the city onto the west side of Union Bridge built high over the Denburn, which is now confined to an underground culvert. This irrevocably altered the pattern of road traffic to the south and west of the city. A number of roads from earlier times are largely still on the ground but have become incorporated into modern city streets.

In Aberdeen the historic route to the south left the old city centre at the Green and headed west by Windmill Brae and Langstane Place, a route which can still be followed. It took this slightly circuitous line to avoid wet areas near the River Dee, which at that time covered a wide estuary in what is now the Aberdeen Harbour area. These wet areas have long disappeared, having been reclaimed for the railway and harbour developments. The route then turns south on to the Hardgate as it runs parallel to Holburn Street to the old Bridge of Dee and uses the Causey Mounth road to reach Stonehaven and beyond. The name Hardgate is explained by G. M. Fraser in his book *Aberdeen Street Names*. It means the hard or "made" road, gate (or gait) being an old Scots word for a road or street. Obviously, it must have been of importance to be publicly noted as a "made" road. As the Hardgate headed south it passed the end of what is now Nellfield Place, and here the Old

Deeside Road diverged and began its route to the west. When Holburn Street was developed as the new route to the south from the west end of Union Street it severed the Hardgate from the Old Deeside Road. Holburn Street ran straight through the junction of the two older roads.

Further separation of the two old roads took place in the 20th century. This was due to the construction of Great Southern Road as another new route to the south, crossing the line of the old Hardgate, and obliterating a short section of it. More recently a major roundabout development on the junction of Great Southern Road and Holburn Street has further obscured the origins of the Old Deeside Road, and also its junction with the southbound Hardgate. However, despite the development of a modern road system and increased traffic it is still possible to glimpse something of the past before heading further along the route.

Figure 1A shows the modern Great Southern Road roundabout which sits where the Old Deeside Road parted from the Hardgate (NJ 931 051). While the old buildings in the foreground of Figure 1 have gone, the rooflines of the two buildings behind can still be identified, although the rightmost one appears to have an addition into the roof.

Moving forward a little, the Old Deeside Road can still be found as Broomhill Road, which was developed on the line of the old route. While it is now a pleasant street with houses, a school and a church dating from the 19th and 20th centuries, it was actually the main commercial route heading to and from Deeside destinations long before that. Fraser adds some context to this area by describing the small estates on the edge of the city, with their houses which preceded this development. The main estate was Pitmuckston or Pitmuxton, latterly known as Pitstruan, which dated from 1309 when Robert the Bruce granted it to Hugo, a cleric of Aberdeen.

To its west was the estate of Broomhill, more recently created in the 18th century as an offshoot of the Ruthrieston lands nearer the River Dee. The Hardgate runs through the Ruthrieston area to the old Bridge of Dee.

Figure 1: Last house on Old Deeside Road, Hardgate, 1917.

Figure 1A: Start of the Old Deeside Road, Hardgate, Aberdeen.

Figure A is a view of Broomhill Road looking west. Fraser mentions the "new" Ruthrieston church which is seen in the distance (NJ 925 043).

Where Broomhill Road ends at the bridge over the former Deeside railway, Auchinyell Road takes over and maintains the route over Kaimhill and down to Garthdee Road. Auchinyell Road is a busy bus and commuter route running through 20th century housing. However, it still follows the line of the old road, winding over the hill through what was once farmland.

Figure A: Broomhill Road with the church in the distance.

Fraser notes that the road was widened and improved as far back as the mid 19th century, but in his day it was still open farmland prior to major housing developments in the 20th century. Fraser mentions the "Two-mile Cross" which had been a prominent marker on the old road hereabouts, being two miles from the city centre, but now sadly long gone. It dated back to at least the 1640s when the Duke of Montrose visited the city. The City Council has retained the name in a street here as a historic link to times past. In spite of all the changes in this area of the city the road is still recognisable, and some of the wall on the left of Fraser's Figure 2 at Auchinyell Bridge remains on the site. Figure 2 from Fraser's book shows what is now Auchinyell Road running through farmland.

In Figure 2A, the view west from Auchinyell Bridge is replicated, with the old road line heading uphill and the former railway on the right now the Deeside Way. The photo is taken from the original bridge over the railway which destroyed a short section of the old road (NJ 921 039). It might be wondered why the road climbs the hill only to drop again to meet Garthdee Road, rather than following the apparently easier and lower route which the former rail line took through a small valley to Pitfodels. The answer is that in times past the low lying area was a boggy hollow with a dark secret. An early Menzies laird of Pitfodels was found dead in the bog, called "The Clash", which had once occupied that area. He was a wizard and his cat had ferociously attacked him as he rode home on his horse one night on the old road. The ghostly cat, with blood dripping from its fangs, is said to haunt that section of the Old Deeside Road, as told by Fenton Wyness in his book *Royal Valley*. As far as I know, no recent sightings have been reported of this alarming beast.

Once over the hill on Auchinyell Road the old road descends to join Garthdee Road which comes from the Bridge of Dee past Robert Gordon University. It is interesting to note that on General Roy's military map of 1747-52 it is the precursor of Garthdee Road which appears to be the route to Cults from the Bridge of Dee, with no sign of the Old Deeside Road. Fraser notes that what is now Garthdee Road was developed in the 1860's without mentioning Roy's map.

The next section towards Morison's Bridge over the Dee at Cults loses the old road as Fraser states it was replaced by the current road. This was built slightly to the north of the earlier road, through to Inchgarth Farm, now converted to houses (NJ 901 029).

Figure 2: Old Deeside Road, Auchinyell Bridge, 1921.

Figure 2A: View west from Auchinyell Bridge.

The old road was subsumed under the gardens of the large houses, developed in the mid 19th century along the bank overlooking the Dee, and must be presumed as destroyed in that process. The developers removed the old road and replaced it apparently without seeking any permission or receiving any objections.

At Inchgarth the old road reappears and heads down to the river bank at Morison's Bridge, known as the Shakkin' Briggie as it had a serious sway on the footway when still in use. It is now a wreck, having gone out of use as a crossing, and consists of little more than uprights for the former suspension bridge. Figure B illustrates the Old Deeside Road, now Inchgarth Road, as it runs west to Morison's Bridge over the River Dee at the bend in the distance (NJ 899 027). The bridge was named after the local church minister who funded it for ease of his parishioners, who crossed to the church on the south side of the river.

Figure B: The view west along Inchgarth Road.

From here the old road turns uphill past Loirsbank, which appears to be an old farm building, and then west along the slope above the river floodplain to the entrance to Allan Park. The narrowness of the road at Loirsbank may indicate the width of the old road as a cart track. Up to this point the old road is still a busy commuter route on a tarred road.

After the break in continuity at the Allan Park we begin to see more rural and unsurfaced sections as we move into the countryside from the city.

The rough track Fraser shows in Figure 3 is now a suburban street. The house at the entrance to Allan Park in the trees can still be seen today. In Figure 3A the Old Deeside Road heads west, now named Loirsbank Road, rising above the River Dee floodplain. It enters Allan Park and disappears as it goes out of the photo (NJ 893 026).

Presumably the development of the park obliterated this section of the old road. As the road ran west beyond the Allan Park it would have held to the slope on the north side of the Dee floodplain to avoid the wetter area below.

This section has now disappeared under houses sitting alongside the old rail line between the Allan Park and West Cults Farm. The sense in avoiding the floodplain is still seen in the water-logging of the lower areas of the park in wet weather.

A couple of hundred yards west of Allan Park the line of the road can still be envisaged below the old rail line in a field rising from West Cults Farm to the Deeside Golf Course eastern boundary. It would have taken a line beside a wooded bank to the south of the railway, now the Deeside Way, until it passes through to the golf course at a small dip.

However it appears that the road itself has disappeared under grass on this section. Figure C looks east down the line of the Old Deeside Road towards West Cults Farm (NJ 886 024).

Figure 3: Old Deeside Road east of Allan Park, Cults, 1921.

Figure 3A: Approach to Allan Park from the east, Cults.

The golf course has changed greatly since Fraser's time and has a new club house and car park. But just west of the new club house, alongside a stone dyke, there remains a section of old road with trees lining it which runs to a new housing development. Even in Fraser's time he says this was an isolated section of road and was lost at the western end already. What remains is a short section of single track road with a gravel surface.

Figure C: The line of the road rises from West Cults.

It is now difficult to accurately reproduce Fraser's Figure 4 but many of the elements can be found, namely stone dykes and old trees on this brief section of track. Figure 4A shows the view looking east along the section of old road at the present golf course (NJ 883 023). According to Fraser, the road here was very narrow around the club house area and a system of raising and lowering a flag was adopted by carters as a means of controlling traffic. Looking at the gradient rising from West Cults Farm, it was probably a sensible method to adopt for horse drawn carts to avoid stopping on the hill.

Figure 4: Old Deeside Road at the then Bieldside Golf Club, 1921.

Figure 4A: The view west at Deeside Golf Club.

He then illustrates the next section of road at Powdeggie. Here a building was placed across the line of the old road to block public use once the road had been replaced by the turnpike on the line of the present A93 to the north. Fraser states that there was much public indignation at first, even destruction of the building, but it soon faded, leaving the old road blocked permanently.

His Figure 5 can be reproduced even to the extent of the old tree on the north side of the road still being there almost a century later, as can be seen in Figure 5A. There is now an access road to the left of the photo which bypasses the building and connects through to Newton Dee (NJ 882 022).

West of Powdeggie, following Fraser's description, the old road runs through Newton Dee, which has changed considerably since his time. I expected the old road to have disappeared because of developments on the estate. Such changes would be expected as many of the estates on lower Deeside have seen housing and other developments on them, particularly in the second half of the 20th century.

However, on the west side of Mains of Newton Dee Farm the road continues as an access track to fields, still in fairly good condition (NJ 879 020). It sits between its old stone boundary dykes with a solid but slightly muddy surface reflecting its current usage. Where it stops at a field gate the stone boundary dyke described by Fraser continues west to a small conifer plantation.

The road, with its dyke on one side and an embankment on the other, passes on the north side of the trees quite clearly as a short grassy track and disappears into a couple of arable fields. From the nearby Deeside Way it is not obvious that a historic road still runs parallel only a short distance away.

Figure D shows the remains of the Old Deeside Road clearly running between the trees and the dyke, to the west of Newton Dee, with Murtle just beyond the rise in the ground (NJ 875 019).

Figure 5: Old Deeside Road at Powdeggie Farm, Bieldside, 1921.

Figure 5A: Powdeggie Farm, Bieldside.

Figure D: Old Deeside Road going west to Murtle.

Beyond these arable fields the new and old access avenues to Murtle House are crossed, and a further section of the old road continues below the Deeside Way. It passes the ruins of a saw mill with its mill lade (NJ 872 017), and then ceases again. Although the onward boundary of the fields might be the line the old road followed, as it takes a logical line towards some houses, nothing is seen on the ground. Despite being unsurfaced, this visible section is in good condition and used as access to an old garden area on the estate. Fraser notes that the Murtle Estate dates back to the 12th century. Beyond a couple of fields the Old Deeside Road reappears as Sunert Road, providing access to houses on a tarred surface before being subsumed beneath the railway line. Taking a line west from Sunert Road, beyond the road bridge over the old rail line, there is a short section of what is likely to be the Old

Deeside Road on the north side of the line. It follows a curve from the Deeside Way, marked by a stone dyke and a row of ash trees, to a level section of a burn just before it drops away under the old railway and into a steep den (NJ 865 015). The line of ash trees is seen in Figure E.

Figure E: Line of ash trees west of Sunert Road.

However, any evidence of the actual road surface is probably buried under the rough vegetation and no sign is seen of it alongside the trees. Presumably this is where the road crossed the burn, as below this point it runs in a steep gorge down to the River Dee floodplain. From here the road appears to have kept a little north of what is now the former rail line towards the old Four Mile House. This can be seen on Taylor and Skinner's map of 1776. Fraser states that the Four Mile House was called Glasterberry. Glasterberry is now a more modern house of the same name. Beside it a burn runs down into a pronounced ravine and Fraser notes that Glasterberry was probably the best place to cross this burn.

Figure 6: Pittengullies Farm, Milltimber, a former inn, 1921.

Figure 6A: The remains of the old access bridge at Pittengullies.

Figure 7: Inch of Culter Ferry, looking east, 1921.

Figure 7A: Location of the Inch of Culter Ferry.

Figure 8: Inch of Culter Ferry houses, 1921.

Figure 8A: Inch of Culter houses seen from Pittengullies.

At this point Fraser mentions that Glasterberry was at the junction of the Old Deeside Road and what he called the Candyglirach road. This latter road met the Old Deeside Road by coming down from Culter House, which is about a mile to the north-west. He seems to imply that the Candyglirach road had some history, but does not elaborate at this stage. Further detail of this road emerges once progress along the Old Deeside Road reaches the Park Estate.

The line of the Old Deeside Road on Taylor and Skinner's map continues past a house which would be either Milltimber Farm or Pittengullies on the outskirts of Peterculter. From there the old road ran into the village itself on the line of the railway. Fraser's Figure 6 shows Pittengullies as it was in his day, but it is now the site of a modern housing development with no trace of the old house remaining, as can be seen in Figure 6A (NJ 849 007). The abutments of the old access bridge to fields on the south side of the railway appear to be the only clue now remaining.

Below Pittengullies the old ferry across the River Dee used to ply at the Inch of Culter (NJ 848 006). The scene captured by Fraser's Figure 7 can almost be replicated from the riverside footpath just west of Pittengullies. Figure 7A shows the scene by the riverside today. Fraser states that the ferry was well used in the summer, but only occasionally in the winter. However, the marker tree he identified as a guide for the ferryman has gone, although some large tree stumps by the riverside may mark its former site.

Fraser shows the ferry cottages at the Inch of Culter in Figure 8. The location by the river has continued as the setting for the more modern buildings which must have replaced the old cottages on the site. Figure 8A shows the scene today (NJ 848 006).

As Fraser explains in his book, the old road disappeared with the development of the railway line in the immediate area, but some of the locations included in his description can still be found as reminders of the historic road.

Once Culter Station is reached the Old Deeside Road can be picked up again, a little below the A93 as it enters the village. The old road touches the A93 and then makes a turn to the south, to continue up Deeside on its original route through what is now quiet countryside.

Chapter 2

Peterculter to Banchory

Map 2 from Cults to Drumoak covers the first few miles of this section, with Map 3 from Drumoak to Banchory covering the remainder of the old road in this area.

To the west of the former Culter Station the Old Deeside Road can be found on the north side of the old railway (NJ 837 005). The name Culter refers to the village of Peterculter. There is also Maryculter on the south side of the River Dee which usually gets its full name. The Old Deeside Road west of Culter Station is a suburban street with some older houses on the north side and newer houses on the south side. These newer houses were built on the railway sidings for Culter Paper Mill, now itself replaced by a housing development beside the Culter Burn just to the west. Therefore the old road must have marked the edge of the sidings, before rising up a short distance to meet the A93 almost at the Malcolm Road junction. Just as it meets the A93 it turns off to the south and drops to a sharp corner to the left. It now descends to cross the Culter Burn by an awkwardly set bridge and heads west out of the village. Figure 9A shows the bridge over the Culter Burn, only a little more overgrown in comparison to Fraser's Figure 9 (NJ 835 005). The access to replicate Fraser's photograph is on overgrown steep ground above the burn and is not recommended.

In Figure F the Culter Burn is seen in its attractive gorge below the old road bridge in the village of Peterculter (NJ 835 005). If it seems strange that a relatively small burn runs in such a substantial gorge, then the history of the Culter Burn provides some answers. The Deeside Field Club published journals over a number of years, covering aspects of Deeside and surrounding areas.

Figure 9: Bridge over the Culter Burn, 1921.

Figure 9A: Bridge over the Culter Burn from the west.

In the 1935 edition of *The Deeside Field* there is an article on The Lochs of the Dee Basin, by Alex Bremner. In his article he describes how at the end of the most recent ice age the area to the northwest of Peterculter held large bodies of glacial melt water. The Loch of Skene is a small reminder of this era according to the article. The melt water flowing down both the Gormack and Leuchar Burns joined to form the Culter Burn about a mile west of the village. This post glacial watercourse had sufficient power to cut the gorge into the solid rock, which remains today as a reminder of the volumes of water which once shaped the local countryside.

Figure F: The Culter Burn gorge from the bridge.

The old road continues from the bridge over the Culter Burn as a minor public road heading west to pass Kennerty Farm, a dairy which was well known in the 20th century.

It continues for about half a mile to Coalford. At the road junction the Old Deeside Road turns left, and beyond the former railway runs for another mile to the Dalmaik crossroads (NO 809 988).

Coalford was to be the junction from where a railway would run across country to Alford, but it never came to fruition. From Coalford to Dalmaik the Old Deeside Road is well-signed as the Deeside Way and is a narrow road on a fairly straight line.

An interesting feature on this section of the road is a track going into a conifer plantation on the north side of the road. This track heads north at right angles to the road.

The trees in Fraser's Figure 11 have been replaced by the conifer plantation but the road line has been preserved as an access track. This was the original approach road to Drum Castle from the Old Deeside Road prior to the turnpike development further north, now the A93.

Figure 11A shows the current scene where the former access road to Drum Castle heads north from the Old Deeside Road (NO 816 992). From the north side of the plantation the access track is overgrown. A short section can still be found north of the old rail line where a track heads west beside the SSPCA Animal Rescue Centre. This track meets the minor road, which was formerly the Drum Station road, just south of the A93.

The area has other historical interest, with Normandykes Roman Camp just over the hill to the south of the old road. The Temple Burn runs in the small valley below the road, a reminder of when the Knights Templar were landowners here with their headquarters across the Dee at Maryculter.

Figure 11: The old Drum Castle entrance road, Dalmaik, 1921.

Figure11A: The old approach to Drum Castle.

Figure 12: Old Deeside Road, Dalmaik Crossroads, Drumoak, 1921.

Figure 12A: Dalmaik Crossroads, looking east.

At Dalmaik crossroads the old road continues west for a short distance as a tarred access road to houses and then becomes a gravel path as part of the Deeside Way route. As it leaves Dalmaik crossroads it passes over what appears to be an old bridge at Cadgerford, which Fraser estimates to date from the early 19th century. Given its name it must have replaced an earlier ford over the burn at this point. A cadger is a Scots word for an itinerant dealer or carter and may suggest a long history to the ford. The road heading south from the crossroads leads to Dalmaik Church ruins by the River Dee. This is named after St Maik or St Mazota, said to have arrived from Ireland in the 6th century with St Bride or Bridget.

Figure 12A, as the modern version of Fraser's Figure 12, is taken from the old road, slightly to the right of the original, as Fraser's likely location is now in the garden of a house. However, the scene is remarkably similar to the original view. Both photographs are taken looking east at the crossroads (NO 809 988).

The next section of the old road has been made up into a gravel path as part of the Deeside Way as it curves round a northerly bend in the River Dee, but even in Fraser's time he described it as "a mere path". It still passes through an area of broom and whins, flowering yellow in early summer as he notes. At this point the Deeside Way follows a northward route which was the Kirk Road. The view along the Kirk Road towards the A93 is shown in Figure G (NO 801 988). This led worshippers from the higher ground of Drumoak parish, above where the A93 now passes through the area, down to the old church near the river. Subsequently, the newer church on the hillside above the A93 replaced the need for both this road and the old church.

The path then heads west to pick up the Old Deeside Road beyond the former manse (NO 797 988). Fraser states that the manse and its grounds were built on the line of the old road. The section beyond the manse leads to the public road running from Drumoak to the Park Bridge over the Dee and is easily followed as the Deeside Way. At first it continues as a gravel path by a pond, but then becomes an unsurfaced access track. Modern leisure walking has brought this part of the old road into more frequent use, but many walkers may not appreciate that they are travelling along this historic route from the 18th century and possibly earlier.

Figure G: The old Kirk Road at Drumoak.

On the west side of the public road a service road leads to East Park Farm which seems to fit Fraser's description as the continuation of the Old Deeside Road. It appears in Fraser's writing as Bakebare Farm (NO 793 982).

However, investigation into the edge of the plantation on the north side of the access road shows that the Old Deeside Road sat a little to the north, and can still be found as a path in the woodland with its boundary embankments.

Figure H: Old Deeside Road at East Park Farm.

The view of the Old Deeside Road looking east along the road with its embankments is shown in Figure H (NO 793 982). The old road eventually turns to the north a little before reaching the farm, and disappears into arable fields on the Park Estate, as it did in Fraser's time.

Within the Park Estate Fraser notes that the only reminder of the road is the Lime Walk, as seen in Figure I, which appears to follow the line of the Old Deeside Road. The road line appears to continue along the west avenue (NO 778 976). This section can still be walked with the Old Deeside Road fitting into a designed estate landscape. He then has the old road run along the north end of a field, but that has been lost through quarry operations, although across the ditch from the Park West Lodge there remains a short section of undisturbed hard ground which may be a last vestige of the old road in this area (NO 770 971).

Fraser states that by 1807 this section of the Old Deeside Road had gone out of use apart from local access, with changes after 1822 on the estate obliterating most of the evidence of the old road. Worthy of note is the house of West Park, once the old Park Inn for travellers on Deeside. Just west of here stood the toll house, now gone, at the end of the first section of the Deeside turnpike of 1798.

Figure I: Old Deeside Road as the Park Lime Walk.

In this area it is possible to pick up the story relating to the Candyglirach road mentioned by Fraser at Glasterberry, near Murtle. The Candyglirach road as seen on the Taylor and Skinner map only goes as far as

Culter House from Glasterberry. But in the Park area, Fraser provides more information on Candyglirach. On the OS maps Candyglirach appears as the name of a farm north of Park. Fraser says that this was one of the ancient lands of the Drum Forest, granted to Burnard of Leys (now Crathes) by Robert Bruce. Fraser derives the name from Ceann-de-Cleireach, or head of the clerk or clergyman. This is not a very clear derivation unless it means the head of the land held by the clergyman. In a website, *Old Roads of Scotland*, the place name is included in a charter of 1247 to the Burnett of Leys family as Kilmaclerauche.

The website address of this most interesting history resource is at www.oldroadsofscotland.com/miscmedaberdeen.htm#drumoak and is worth visiting. As "kil" in Gaelic usually refers to a religious establishment, this might make more sense in relation to the clergyman. Fraser at this point refers to the Candyglirach road, but unfortunately not in any detail.

It may be that the road from Glasterberry continued past Culter House and, keeping to the north of the Culter Burn's deep channel at Peterculter, headed west through the Anguston area towards Candyglirach. This is perhaps a clue to another section of ancient road along the Dee valley. Fraser's main reason for discussing the Candyglirach road here is in relation to another old road in this area, called the Couper Road. This is essentially the extension of the Cryne Corse Mounth pass on to the north side of the River Dee. The Mounth pass would have led from the south to a ford near the Kirkton of Durris which is on the south bank of the Dee. Fraser notes that the part of the Couper Road near the river and turnpike had disappeared. But he describes the remainder of it as the minor public road running north by the Loch of Park, Collonach, crossing the Candyglirach road, and reaching West Cullerley where five roads meet. It then goes by Finnarcy and Echt onwards to Kintore and Inverurie. As one of the meanings of Couper in Scots is a trader, it is reckoned to reflect the traffic using it in former times. As a major link to the south via the Cryne Corse Mounth it would have seen numerous livestock traders and drovers using it, coming from the various markets in the eastern part of Aberdeenshire.

Moving back to the Old Deeside Road, Fraser states that the road has disappeared from the West Lodge of Park until the road leading from the A93 down to Crathes Bridge over the Dee is met. But with the conversion of the railway to a walkway the likely road line to the south of the railway by the old Mills of Drum is probably better seen than in Fraser's day when the railway was in use. The old road then turned north, was crossed by the rail line and went through the grounds of the houses on the east side of Crathes where it has since disappeared.

However, its possible emergence onto the Crathes Bridge road as the entrance to Woodbank is still there (NO 749 964). Opposite there Fraser sees it going through the wood to Crathes Station as a path, but that has disappeared under a conifer plantation.

The next visible section of the old road is on the Deeside Way, running as a gravel track by Milton Cottage and on towards Milton of Crathes.

The Old Crathes Bridge at Milton, which takes the Old Deeside Road across the Coy Burn running down from Crathes Estate (NO 743 962), is one of the oldest remaining features of the road, and Fraser dates it to at least the early 1700s. It is the only remaining complete bridge along the length of the road. It still crosses the burn, as seen in Figure 13A, where it is overshadowed by the later railway bridge, and the A93 bridge, dating from 1939.

North, beyond the A93, the old turnpike bridge is concealed in trees at Crathes East Lodge. Thus there are four bridges here illustrating the history of Deeside travel through at least three centuries.

Fraser makes reference to the sharp corner on the turnpike road which can still be found opposite the East Lodge of Crathes Castle where the turnpike bridge crosses the Coy Burn. He notes that this was a very awkward bend, and subsequently the 1939 bridge must have been built to reduce the risks to travellers.

Figure 13: Old Deeside Road bridge at Crathes, 1921.

Figure 13A: Old Crathes Bridge.

The scene at Old Crathes Bridge now has more trees and shrubs than was the case in Fraser's photo in Figure 13. Cattle no longer roam the area as they obviously did earlier in the 20th century and the modern walker on the route should have unobstructed access over the bridge.

The view through the old railway bridge in his Figure 14 now has a softer and gentler feel than the rather stark scene in Fraser's photo, as shown in Figure 14A (NO 743 962). This is probably caused by the former management of trees and bushes by the line side to prevent fires from sparks emitted by steam trains. It is easily accessed by a track from the entrance to Crathes Castle, or by footpath from Milton of Crathes.

From this old bridge the follower of the Old Deeside Road must now move to the eastern outskirts of modern Banchory before meeting another interesting section of road. There is a part of the old road running down by the graveyard as the A93 enters Banchory from the east, illustrated in Figure J (NO 706 957).

In the old graveyard a notable feature is the mort-house. Its function was to keep bodies safe from resurrectionists. These were criminals who stole fresh corpses for medical research from the latter years of the 18th century until 1832 when legal methods of procuring bodies were created. Once the body had decomposed it was no longer of medical interest and could be buried safely in a grave.

The Old Deeside Road here is an isolated section of tarred street as it runs down to what were the engine sheds for the railway, seen on the left in Figure J. The Old Deeside Road then disappears. Before the railway and turnpike were developed the centre of Banchory was in this low area of ground. The construction of the bridge over the Dee, west of the old village centre in 1799, began the process of replacing the old village. The extension of the turnpike through Banchory in 1802, on the line of the current A93, led to the development of the modern centre of Banchory and essentially consigned the old road and village to history.

Figure 14: Crathes Bridge viewed under rail bridge, 1921.

Figure 14A: View under Crathes rail bridge to the old road bridge.

Figure J: Old Deeside Road entering Banchory.

An interesting feature of the turnpike development is related on an inscribed stone set into the wall on the north side of the A93 just west of this section. When the turnpike was being made in 1802 a burial cist was uncovered, containing an urn with cremation ashes. This was commemorated in 1923 by Banchory Town Council who had two stones set into the wall. The stones are from the burial and one of them carries an inscription on it which reads; "These stones formed part of a prehistoric short cist, which containing an urn was discovered here when the highway was made about 1800. An early Celtic wheel cross probably from St. Ternan's churchyard is built into the manse wall opposite. Recorded by the Provost and Town Council of Banchory 1923." The cist stone is shown in Figure K. The Celtic wheel cross stone is also still in place across the road, built into the wall by the roadside.

Fraser claims that a road running west from Dee Street, named Bridge Street, was the Old Deeside Road, and it does follow a reasonable line from where the old village was located (NO 695 955). These appear to be the only parts of the road still existing in Banchory and are now seen as town streets rather than a historic highway from the past.

Figure K: Cist stone on the turnpike line at Banchory.

At the western extremity of Banchory where Fraser states the road ran on the south side of the A93, it has now disappeared because of residential development. However, where the last part of the likely line of the road might have been, careful observation of an area of trees shows the faint line of what looks like a track emerging from the housing and joining the A93, perhaps a last shadow of the old road on the landscape (NO 680 961).

Chapter 3

Banchory to Aboyne

Map 4 from Banchory to Kincardine O'Neil and Map 5 from Kincardine O'Neil to Aboyne cover this section of the old road.

After the possible exit of the old road from Banchory, seen as a faint mark on the ground, nothing is now visible until Bridge of Canny. As in Fraser's day, the Old Deeside Road turns off the A93 to the north and continues as a minor public road until it meets the B993 road from Torphins to Kincardine O'Neil. The scene here has changed little in nearly a century apart from the updating of the road itself and the loss of the old fingerpost sign on the left in Figure 15. Figure 15A shows the Old Deeside Road leaving the modern A93 at Bridge of Canny (NO 652 971).

The Old Deeside Road here has excellent views of the countryside as it crosses higher ground than the A93, which follows the Dee valley. It is shorter than the A93 from here to Kincardine O'Neil as the 1802 turnpike was built to follow the river to link with the old ford at Inchbare, and its replacement, the Potarch Bridge. On the old road just beyond Craiglash Quarry there is a crossroads (NO 618 988) with an old route from the ford at Inchbare on the Dee, and Potarch Bridge, to Craigmyle at Torphins.

The track down to Potarch is an easy and pleasant walk worth visiting for the Warlock Stone. The onward road to Craigmyle is rather lost in a conifer plantation on the north side of the road, although its start can still be seen on the ground. The moorland area to the north is called Moss Maud and the drove road across it was patrolled by the "Heidless Horseman" who terrified travellers into a horrible death in the treacherous moss. This tale is recounted by Fenton Wyness in his book *Royal Valley*.

Figure 15: Old Deeside Road, Bridge of Canny, 1921.

Figure 15A: Glassel road leaves the A93 at Bridge of Canny.

The Warlock Stone and nearby Bog-loch of Sluie were at the centre of Deeside witchcraft in the 16th century, with the stone being the main focus of a coven of witches. The Warlock Stone is off the Old Deeside Road just west of Craiglash Quarry, on the old route to Potarch mentioned above.

The Bog-loch sits just below the Old Deeside Road a little way east of the quarry and still retains an atmosphere about it. Fenton Wyness provides an interesting background to the local witchcraft cult. Witchcraft trials were held in Aberdeen in 1596-7 and Wyness states that twenty three women and one man were convicted and condemned to death. Some took their own lives, which might be understandable given the alternatives, where several were strangled by the hangman, and then dragged through the streets until they were unrecognisable. The majority were burnt at the stake in Aberdeen, and this was a popular public attraction of its day.

Disability was no barrier as Wyness quotes six shillings (thirty pence) expenditure for a barrow to carry a cripple witch, presumably to her death. The old Scottish protection against witchcraft was to plant a rowan tree near the front door of the house. Across Deeside, in the present day, old rowans can still be seen near ruined farms.

Fraser's Figure 17 and Figure 17A both illustrate the Old Deeside Road heading east at the junction with the B993 near Kincardine O'Neil (NO 607 991). While the views are similar, road conditions have changed considerably over the ninety year gap.

After meeting the B993 the Old Deeside Road heads west on the south side of the entrance to Kincardine Lodge, going through a field gate and following the south edge of the trees to Borrowstone Farm (NO 603 991). It is a clear grassy track along this section as seen in Figure L.

From here there used to be a section downhill towards Kincardine O'Neil, along the wood edge. I was told that it had in recent years been ploughed to include it in the field, which was regrettable, as it had been a good short cut to the village.

Figure 17: Old Deeside Road near Kincardine O'Neil, 1921.

Figure 17A: The Junction with the Torphins road near Kincardine O'Neil.

Figure L: Old Deeside Road near Borrowstone.

Going through Kincardine O'Neil village some traces of the Old Deeside Road can be seen at the Old Smiddy, where a line of houses continues straight on following the line of the old road. The continuation of the old road line is blocked by the church and manse. The original exit from the village has now disappeared under cultivation.

The next obvious section is a short grassy track which emerges onto the A93 at Heughhead about half a mile to the west of the village. Figure M shows this section of the Old Deeside Road heading west to Heughhead (NO 584 999). From here about one and a half miles have to be travelled to the west to find the old road again as it carries straight on at Newton of Drumgesk, while the A93 turns to the north following the turnpike line (NO 563 996). This section runs in a very straight line and is an excellent walk.

It starts as an unsurfaced track with a short overgrown section at Drumgesk which is easily passable. From there the road continues in good condition to cross the Belwade road and rise gently towards Aboyne as a grassy track.

Figure M: Old Deeside Road at Heughhead, Kincardine O'Neil.

There is a short section where the road becomes a footpath but it is soon passed and becomes a clear track again along the north side of Bell Wood. At the corner of Bell Wood it gets lost in new housing at the east edge of Aboyne. Figure N shows the descent west into Aboyne with the Dee valley beyond. The modern A93 comes into the village from the right of the photo by the trees and buildings in the middle distance (NO 546 991). It is an easy route to follow and provides good views from higher ground than the A93, particularly across to Mortlich Hill north of Aboyne. New housing and other developments in Aboyne have altered Fraser's description of the Tarland Burn crossing, but Low Road running into the former station square appears to follow the old road line into the centre of Aboyne. At this point Fraser states that the A93 leaving Aboyne to the west runs on the old road line as far as Heughhead about a mile west of the village.

Figure N: Old Deeside Road descending into Aboyne.

Fraser makes interesting observations about the old routes on Deeside prior to the development of modern Aboyne. The original local settlement was further east beyond the Loch of Aboyne, where the OS 1:25,000 map shows church remains (NJ 541 001). There would have been no need for the road to go to the modern location of Aboyne as the other focal point in the area was Aboyne Castle to the north. Fraser points to the likelihood of the old road in front of the castle linking through Allach Wood to the road just travelled at the Bell Wood. However the old Kirktown east of the loch is not on this road line. Might this imply that the Old Deeside Road route described via Drumgesk post-dates the movement of Aboyne to its current location as this straight route bypasses the old settlement near the loch. It may be that there was an older road line through the former Kirktown. Figure O shows the view of Aboyne Castle from the potential old road north of the present village (NO 526 992).

Figure O: Aboyne Castle from possible old road.

With regard to the earlier Aboyne and its old roads, Fraser puts forward the view that the east-west track running in front of the castle and continuing beyond the Aboyne to Tarland road for a short distance could be a Deeside Road from before 1760, now remaining as a tarred drive in the eastern part (NO 526 992). Figure P illustrates this possible Deeside Road, which may predate 1760, on the west side of the Tarland road. Now a farm track, it disappears into fields at the far end of the road (NO 518 992).

Figure P: Possible Deeside Road from before 1760, near Aboyne.

This description has a logical basis to it, but any link from the old location of Aboyne east of the loch would have disappeared when the golf course was developed. However it is an interesting observation on the development of the village over the centuries, with its various connections into the Deeside road system apparently persisting throughout the period.

Chapter 4

Aboyne to Ballater

Map 6 from Aboyne to Cambus o' May and Map 7 from Cambus o' May to Coilacriech cover this section of the old road.

From Aberdeen to Aboyne the modernisation from the Old Deeside Road to the turnpike took place as one change. The turnpike developments were in two phases; in 1798 to Mills of Drum and 1802 to Aboyne. West of Aboyne the old road was firstly treated as a commutation road until 1855 when it became a turnpike. Fraser states that this causes some complications in deciding which phase of development some sections of the old road could belong to, as each development had divergences from the previous. Beyond Balmoral the old military road provides a further layer of history. Other than the possible road from earlier than 1760 at Aboyne Castle, the next obvious section of Old Deeside Road is about half a mile west of Heughhead where the A93 takes a slight turn to the south just before the gliding field (NO 495 988). At this turn the line of the Old Deeside Road can just be seen heading straight on towards Ferrar in Figure Q. Even in Fraser's time he states it was disused and overgrown.

However, if a line is taken keeping to the drier and slightly raised bank on the right, eventually a stone dyke is found. This runs west towards Ferrar, probably showing the old road line as it approached the house. The overgrown section east of that dyke rising from the A93 holds a clue to the route of the old road.

The route appears to run in part along a distinctly straight line of broom bushes, as seen in Figure R looking east towards the A93 (NO 490 989), possibly showing a change of soil conditions left by the old road.

Figure Q: Old Deeside Road towards Ferrar.

Further clarity on the line of the Old Deeside Road here can be gained from another old road. Where the Old Deeside Road leaves the A93 just before the gliding field an old road heading north to Braeroddach takes a higher line round the hill of Craig Ferrar (NO 488 994). The Braeroddach road is now only a footpath and eventually runs into thick undergrowth further up the track. However, as it climbs it does provide a good perspective of the line of the Old Deeside Road heading for Ferrar, and its probable link with the stone dyke.

Fraser thought that the neglected state of this section of the Old Deeside Road, even in his day, was due to it being part of the road which pre-dated the commutation road. He reckons the commutation road was the basis of the turnpike and the present A93, which all bypass Ferrar on what was then a new road line.

Figure R: Broom bushes showing road line.

Although the road has now disappeared, these clues in the landscape show some evidence of its history. The reason for the old road going by Ferrar was that it had been the residence of one of the Earl of Huntly's family in the 16th century. The current house, however, only dates from the 19th century. West of Ferrar, Fraser states that the old road is more easily seen than to the east. Unfortunately the section between Ferrar and Boghead to the west is now a conifer plantation where the ground has been ploughed before planting. No evidence remains of this section of the old road which ran through to meet the A93 again before the Dinnet Burn is crossed.

The next visible section of the old road is at Mill of Dinnet, a little east of the village itself. Here Fraser notes the lack of a bridge on the Old Deeside Road abutments. These abutments are located on the other side of the old rail line from the A93 and show the former crossing point on the Dinnet Burn. At some date since his time a new bridge has been built, using the old abutments. This now forms a third bridge over the Dinnet Burn along with both the A93 and former rail bridges sitting to its north (NO 469 990), as shown in Figure S.

Interesting remains of mill lades can be found adjacent to the old road where it crosses the Dinnet Burn. Beyond the bridge the Old Deeside Road can still be traced coming under the rail bridge and merging onto the A93 as a grassy track beside the burn.

Figure S: Mill of Dinnet Bridge on old abutments.

Figure T shows the view from above taken from the old rail line, now the Deeside Way (NO 468 990). Fraser has the old road continuing for another 100 yards or so to the west, but A93 improvements have removed that evidence over the years.

Fraser mentions another old road at the Mill of Dinnet which can still be walked and is a historic cross country route. Across the A93 from Mill of Dinnet a track marked "St James" heads north. At first it is a tarred access to houses but soon becomes a grassy track which eventually crosses a low hill and descends past Tillyhermack Farm onto the B9119 near Tarland. It is an old drove road, which was the first dry road on the east side of the Muir of Dinnet. It accessed a ford on the Dee to link with the Firmount road on the Glen Tanar Estate, heading for the south as a livestock route.

Figure T: Old Deeside Road at Dinnet Burn.

The old drove road passes by Mulloch Hill. There is a large cairn on the summit which has a traditional story associated with it. This is quoted in *A New History of Aberdeenshire*, written by Alexander Smith, and published in 1875. The tradition is that this was where a Danish king or general fell in a battle. Sadly, it appears to be unfounded.

Referring back to the old Firmounth pass, the monument set up by Sir William Brooks near Tillycairn still sits by the roadside, as seen in Figure 10A (NO 473 973). It now has more lichens growing on it than in Fraser's time when it is seen in his Figure 10. It is easily accessed by the sign-posted Firmounth road from the memorial at Cobbleheugh, or by a better track from Oldhall to Tillycairn.

No trace of the Old Deeside Road now exists through Dinnet until the western edge of the village is reached, where the A93 turns slightly to the north. On the left, looking over an old gravel pit, a narrow clear line can be seen through the conifers which is the old road heading onwards across the Muir of Dinnet towards Cambus o' May (NO 455 985).

Figure U illustrates the line of the Old Deeside Road as it leaves Dinnet village.

From Dinnet the old road runs north of, and roughly parallel to, the Deeside Way (the former rail line) for some distance as a heathery track through the trees, although it eventually becomes a bit overgrown for easy walking. Along its line the boundary dykes can still be seen protruding from the undergrowth.

Fraser states that this section used to be a popular walk, but the old rail line now provides that function on a better surface, even if there is less cultural history attached to it.

Figure U: Old Deeside Road leaving Dinnet.

Beyond this older unused section an estate track for Dinnet House comes from the A93 to the north and the Old Deeside Road becomes a good stone surfaced access track on the south side of the old rail line. Figure V shows this section of the old road used as the Dinnet Estate track (NO 434 975).

Figure 10: Memorial on the Firmounth, Tillycairn, Dinnet, 1921.

Figure 10A: Firmounth memorial, near Dinnet.

Figure V: Old Deeside Road by the former rail line.

After about a mile it passes under the old railway line onto the north side again and continues as an attractive route through birch woodland to Cambus o' May Station.

Fraser's Figure 18 shows a typical stretch of the old road east of Cambus o' May Station. Using the hill visible in his photograph, but now more obscured by trees, it is possible to make a reasonable guess as to the location. Figure 18A looks east in the approximate area of Fraser's photograph in the birch wood between Dinnet and Cambus o' May. Interestingly, the road surface appears little changed from his time, although he thought it was probably in better condition in his day than when it was the main road in the area.

Figure 18: Old Deeside Road east of Cambus o' May, 1921.

Figure 18A: Between Dinnet and Cambus o' May.

Figure 20: Former Ferry Public House, Cambus o' May, 1921.

Figure 20A: Cutaway Cottage, Cambus o' May, now obscured.

This section from Dinnet to Cambus o' May comprises around three miles of old road, mostly in good condition and essentially all available as an alternative to the old rail line. Fraser states that this is the longest continuous section of the old road still in existence apart from the public road section from Bridge of Canny to Kincardine O'Neil.

From Cambus o' May Station the route coincides with the Deeside Way to pass between Cutaway Cottage and the River Dee. The cottage was once the public house for the nearby ferry over the Dee. It had a corner sliced off to accommodate the railway line in an area restricted by the locally steep ground, hence the interesting name.

The bed of the former rail line has been planted with trees which now obscure Fraser's original view in Figure 20, as can be seen in Figure 20A (NO 419 977). The old rail line forms part of the grounds of the cottage, so that the interesting "cutaway" image has been lost for the meantime. However, the view of the front of the cottage and the riverside section of old road in Figure 21 is much clearer to see and forms part of the modern Deeside Way. It passes between the cottage and the river on a good level section of track, coinciding with the Old Deeside Road. Figure 21A shows the modern view of Cutaway Cottage along the bank of the Dee (NO 419 977).

A little beyond the cottage the Deeside Way turns right onto the former railway line. At this point the Old Deeside Road still exists as a pleasant grassy track by the river and continues ahead to follow a dyke to Turnerhall where the old road reverts to the A93. From this point the A93 replaces the old road until Tullich is reached about a mile further west. Figure W shows the Old Deeside Road by the river west of Cambus o' May. This section is a pleasant alternative to the Deeside Way going towards Turnerhall (NO 417 979).

Tullich was the main settlement in this area on the north side of the River Dee, although little now remains apart from the old ruined church. It was matched by Pannanich on the south side with its mineral wells, which became famous for their health properties.

Figure 21: Old Deeside Road at Cambus o' May, 1921.

Figure 21A: Old road at Cutaway Cottage.

Eventually both settlements were overtaken by the development of Ballater as the main village in the 19th century on a new site beside Craigendarroch Hill. The effect on the old road will be seen in the following paragraphs.

Figure W: Old Deeside Road by the River Dee.

At Tullich the main location to look for the old road is at the bridge over the Tullich Burn just west of the ruined church (NO 387 975). While Fraser was still able to see the abutments of the old bridge over the Tullich Burn on the north side of the A93 bridge, these have now disappeared. He also states that there is no known picture of that old bridge, so everything is now lost.

The traces of the old road have not gone entirely here as just west of the bridge there is a stone dyke running downhill towards the Pass of Ballater junction. This must show the continuation of the road from the old bridge, although it now sits unnoticed among grass and some trees (NO 386 974).

The title of this chapter is now seen to be a modern definition used for convenience. As the Old Deeside Road came into use along this section of Deeside there was no Ballater village, which had yet to be built on moorland by the river. Tullich and Pannanich were the communities on either side of the Dee in the locality. The Old Deeside Road continued west by what is now the Pass of Ballater road and is the logical route before Ballater was built. From here to Bridge of Gairn the Old Deeside Road is easily followed as a good public road running through the steep sided gap to the north of Craigendarroch Hill. There are some interesting remains from earlier times in the Pass of Ballater, particularly the small stone bridge and Fog House close to the north side of the road. These sit below the modern road level on the Ballater Burn, or Loinn Burn. These artefacts were built by William Farquharson of the nearby Monaltrie House, and the remains are still picturesque, although the Fog House is little more than a ruin sitting on a shelf above the burn.. Figure X shows the old Fog House viewed over the Loinn Burn. The road runs level with the top of the ruined house wall.

Figure X: The old Fog House ruins in Pass of Ballater.

Figure 22: The Fog House, Pass of Ballater, c. 1857.

Figure 22A: Fog House
remains at Loinn Burn.

Figure 22 is a photograph of a painting from around 1857, showing the old Fog House in its prime, located in the Pass of Ballater. The current view can be matched mainly by observation of the slanting boulder in the burn in the foreground. Tree growth and the ruined state of the Fog House mean it is difficult to identify in the newer photograph. Unfortunately Figure 22A, which reproduces Figure 22, shows little significant sign of the interesting Fog House remains (NO 371 970). Fraser notes that the bridge provided access to Sgor Buidhe, the hill on the north side of the burn. Here lead and silver were quarried, but latterly building stone, presumably for Ballater, proved more profitable. The Fog House was probably intended as a pleasant picnic spot overlooking the scenic section of the burn. *The Concise Scots Dictionary* gives the derivation of fog as grass, moss or lichen, with a fog house being a small summer house built or lined with mossy turf.

Figure Y shows the old bridge over the Loinn Burn near the Fog House (NO 371 970).

Figure Y: The old Farquharson bridge viewed from the Fog House (NO 371 970).

Chapter 5

The Ballater Area

Map 7 shows the old road in the Ballater area.

While the Old Deeside Road by-passes the village of Ballater itself, Fraser includes some interesting notes about the area.

He mentions a track starting from the Cambus o' May footbridge over the Dee and heading west towards Pannanich. This route is still in existence and is way-marked on good paths to emerge on the South Deeside Road via a fisherman's track by the riverside. On the way it passes below Fraser's view of the Pannanich hamlet in Figure 19. This view has been taken from the South Deeside Road where the hamlet is now signposted as Glascorrie. Although partly obscured by trees the view can still be found but the rightmost cottage in his view has been demolished. Figure 19A shows the old hamlet of Pannanich in a view looking west from the South Deeside Road, with Craigendarroch prominent left of centre (NO 402 971).

At Ballater various bridges crossing the River Dee have come and gone over the past couple of centuries. Fraser's Figure 23 shows the timber bridge which was in use from 1834-1885. This replaced a stone bridge destroyed by the great flood of 1829. The stone bridge had been designed by Thomas Telford who also approved the design of the timber replacement and was more famous for developing the Caledonian Canal. The timber bridge was eventually replaced by the present stone bridge, and the foundations of the timber one can still be seen in the river bed on the downstream side looking like narrow islands. The view which Fraser published is now difficult to replicate because of tree growth. Figure 23A shows the present stone bridge over the Dee at Ballater which is located to the left of the previous timber bridge illustrated by Fraser (NO 372 956).

Figure 19: Old Ford Road, Pannanich, looking west.

Figure 19A: Pannanich with Craigendarroch beyond.

Figure 23: Timber Bridge of Ballater, in use 1834-1885.

Figure 23A: Ballater Bridge in the 21st century.

Fraser's Figure 24 is very difficult to reproduce in a view from the lower slopes of Pannanich Hill as tree growth is now extensive. The best match is taken from a spot below Craig Coillich, at a cleared area above an old quarry on the track leading to Dalmochie lumberjack camp. This is illustrated in Figure 24A viewed from the cleared area noted above (NO 376 956).

Ballater is obviously a lot more developed than in the original photograph, but many of the older buildings still exist in the village.

Dalmochie is worth visiting, where the remains of a Second World War lumber camp are located along with information boards providing further details. This was where the Newfoundland Overseas Forestry Unit had one of numerous camps in Scotland producing timber for the war effort (NO 379 959).

To the west of Ballater, where the A93 meets the Pass of Ballater road, Fraser notes the old 42nd milestone on the Pass road. In his day this stone no longer represented the distance from Aberdeen by the A93, but had been left in place. However, it is no longer there, probably through road improvement over the decades since, as can be seen in the comparison between Figure 25A and Figure 25 (NO 357 969).

The rail line along Deeside, which terminated at Ballater, had been intended to go further up the Dee valley, but primarily as a tramway for timber extraction from the Ballochbuie Forest. Queen Victoria's purchase of that woodland killed off the idea and it was never built, apart from one short section that is now a walk from Ballater to the River Gairn on the line of the old track.

The bridge intended for crossing the Gairn was used as a bridge over the same river about eight miles upstream at Daldownie. The smaller size of the bridge reflects the likely use for a tramway rather than a full scale railway. Figure Z shows the old bridge crossing the Gairn by the ruined farm of Daldownie (NJ 241 008).

Figure 24: Ballater from the hillside south of the Dee, 1856.

Figure 24A: Ballater from the hill to the south of the Dee.

Figure 25: Old 42nd milestone, Pass of Ballater, 1921.

Figure 25A: Site of the old 42nd milestone.

Figure Z: The old bridge at Daldownie, Glen Gairn.

It is a pleasant walk of about four miles alongside the River Gairn from Braenaloin on the B976 near the Gairnshiel military bridge. The B976, running from Crathie to Gairnshiel is largely the old military road. Once it reaches Gairnshiel Bridge the military road becomes the A939 heading towards Corgarff on Donside. However, on the Corgarff side of the pass the old military road cuts off to the west at a right of way sign. This can be followed on foot past a few old military bridges to emerge at Corgarff.

Chapter 6

Ballater to Braemar

Map 7 Cambus o' May to Coilacriech, Map 8 from Coilacriech to Clagganghoul, and Map 9 from Clagganghoul to Braemar cover this section of the old road.

This chapter really starts from the Bridge of Gairn at the west end of the Pass of Ballater, because on the Old Deeside Road, Ballater did not exist, as noted earlier. At the crossing of the River Gairn the present road bridge is the third and southernmost of the crossings taking the Deeside roads across this large tributary of the Dee.

The remains of the other two bridges can be seen upstream of the present bridge but are in a private garden, and so are not accessible by right under the Scottish Outdoor Access Code. I was fortunate to be able to take some photos by kind permission of the property owners for a record of the remains.

In Figure AA the Old Deeside Road retaining walls are seen, located on the east side of the River Gairn. The road descended from right to left down to the bridges of earlier days (NO 352 970).

The retaining wall visible on the east side of the Gairn as it runs downhill to the crossing point is the most easily seen evidence of the old crossings. The old road followed the line of the buildings on the east side of the Gairn, slightly to the north of the A93 and dropped towards the Gairn alongside the retaining wall. According to Fraser the first bridge was a packhorse bridge with awkward angles for anything but horse traffic. This led to the second bridge being built downstream at a place better suited for late

18th century traffic. The present bridge was developed as part of the turnpike road, with the foundation stone laid in 1856.

Figure AA: Old retaining walls at Bridge of Gairn.

Looking from the present bridge the second Deeside road can be seen rising from the River Gairn towards the house as a narrow track in Figure AB (NO 352 971).

From Bridge of Gairn the Old Deeside Road has disappeared under the turnpike and later A93 developments until just west of Coilacriech, where the A93 crosses the Coilacriech Burn on a stone bridge. Beyond the bridge and an open field on the left the old road heads down off the A93 and continues as a grassy track for about half a mile parallel to and slightly below the level of the modern road (NO 319 968).

Figure AB: Old Deeside Road at Bridge of Gairn.

At the west end of this section it emerges through a gate back onto the A93. As Fraser notes, the ruins of earlier dwellings can still be seen beside the track winding through attractive birch woodland. Figure AC shows the remains of old farms on the Coilacriech section of road (NO 318 968). It is still a pleasant walk around 150 years after this section was superseded by the turnpike road.

In Figure AD the old road runs through Coilacriech woodland. Although little noticed, this section is visible from the A93 which passes slightly higher and to the right of the photo.

Figure AC: Old farm near Coilacriech.

From where this section of Old Deeside Road reverts onto the A93, about half a mile requires to be travelled west to find the access road for Rinabaich on the north side of the main road. At this junction another section of the old road can be found. It runs through the gate at the west end of a parking area on the north side of the A93 and provides access on a grass track to some buildings. One of these has been built right on the old road line. Finally it can be seen as a grassy line running downhill towards the A93 where it disappears once more.

Figure AD: Old Deeside Road in Coilacreich woods.

Figure AE shows clearly the Old Deeside Road near Rinabaich. A soft grass track here, it goes unnoticed through a wooded area (NO 304 962). For about two miles no further evidence of the Old Deeside Road is seen until reaching the house named Tomidhu (Fraser names it Tomadhubh) on the north side of the A93 east of Crathie (NO 273 950). At Tomidhu the house remains as in Figure 26 but the small section of road leading off the A93 which Fraser found has deteriorated. Although modernised, the house retains its characteristic style from the past as it sits by the Old Deeside Road passing to its east side. In Figure 26A the old road passes on the right of Tomidhu onto a higher level terrace above the modern A93. The Old Deeside Road climbs past the house and turns west to run along a level bank as a good stone surfaced road to Crathie Church, as seen in Figure AF (NO 268 951).

Figure AE: Old Deeside Road at Rinabaich.

Figure AF: Old Deeside Road near Crathie.

Figure 26: Old Deeside Road, Tomadhubh, Crathie, 1921.

Figure 26A: Tomidhu east of Crathie.

Figure 27: Old Deeside Road behind Crathie Church, 1921.

Figure 27A: Old Deeside Road, Crathie Church looking east.

The old road from Tomidhu emerges from behind Crathie Church as a good access road, much improved from Fraser's time. It passes the church on the north side emerging at the junction of roads between the church and some houses on a bank, as seen in Figure 27. Figure 27A shows the old road running behind Crathie Church. The house on the left and the stone wall on the right both appear in Fraser's photo (NO 264 949). Once past the church the old road holds to the top of the bank on a level section until it descends to meet another old road below it which Fraser calls the coach road. Figure AG shows the Old Deeside Road on top of the bank, with its boundary wall, between Crathie and the B976 (NO 263 950).

Figure AG: Old Deeside Road west of Crathie.

The coach road was developed to accommodate horse coaches as they came into use on the Deeside route. The combined road just above the A93 then leads towards the B976 road junction, although modern improvements have removed the final meeting point. Between Crathie Church and the B976 remains of both old roads are visible but overgrown with some impediment to access by trees.

Fraser notes the interesting timescale on these roads whereby the now disused Post Office was built across the line of the Old Deeside Road. This indicates that the coach road had been developed as the main road before the Post Office was built, and remained the main road until the turnpike was built. The turnpike is now the A93, the lowest of the three roads at Crathie. Beyond the B976 the Old Deeside Road bridge over the Crathie Burn, or at least the remaining south side of its arch, sits in a private garden. It is easily seen from the main road as a picturesque reminder of older times.

The scene at the bridge over the Crathie Burn in Figure 29 has changed little, apart from house modernisation over the decades. Figure 29A shows the old road bridge crossing the Crathie Burn near the B976. Apart from the complete bridge at Crathes (near Banchory), this appears to be the only other remaining fragment of Old Deeside Road bridges (NO 259 952).

From the Crathie Burn to the access track to Newton Farm, and then beyond this to the Lochnalair access road, there appears to be no trace of the old road. However, Fraser describes some evidence of remains on top of the bank above the A93 where the old road appeared to keep to higher ground. This leads the intrepid follower to find some evidence of parts of a level shelf perched above a steep drop onto the A93. While not easy or particularly safe to access, this must be some remnant of the old road sitting invisibly above the modern road "for many generations" as Fraser states.

While interesting to find, it cannot be recommended, as moving around on a steep bank above the A93 is not a safe manoeuvre. It is much easier to pick up the old road just west of this section. At the access track for Lochnalair the Old Deeside Road is easily found running west for a short distance as a farm track parallel to the A93 to meet the old military road. Figure AH illustrates the Old Deeside Road west of Lochnalair running towards the military road (NO 252 953).

Figure 29: Old Deeside Road bridge over the Crathie Burn, 1921.

Figure 29A: Remains of the bridge at Crathie Burn.

Figure AH: Old Deeside Road at Lochnalair.

The military road rises from the A93 and heads north for Glen Gairn and Corgarff, and its junction with the A93 is shown in Figure AI (NO 251 952).

The section of military road between this point and Braemar was built in 1749-53 as part of a longer route from Perthshire to Moray via Glen Shee, Glen Clunie, Deeside, Donside, the Lecht and Tomintoul. Some parts of the Old Deeside Road coincide with the military road but, as will be seen, there are sections which appear to predate the military road and can still be found with relative ease in spite of their age. From the junction with the Lochnalair track the military road heads north to join the B976 from Crathie as it crosses the moors to Gairnshiel. Here the original arched bridge over the River Gairn sits in a very scenic location.

Figure AI: The old military road at the A93.

Fraser includes the Gairnshiel Bridge in Figure 32 as an interesting reminder of the old military roads in the district. It still performs its original function, taking the A939 across the River Gairn over 250 years later, as seen in Figure 32A (NJ 295 008).

Back on Deeside, for the next mile west of the point where the military road leaves the A93, the Old Deeside Road coincides with the current A93 and the former military road until reaching the monument of Cairn na Quheen. This is a stone cairn beside the River Dee which is linked with the Farquharson family. A sign-posted path leads from the A93 layby near Inver down to the old cairn. It also gives access to an interesting section of the Old Deeside Road (NO 239 941).

Figure 32: The old military road bridge, Gairnshiel, 1921.

Figure 32A: Gairnshiel Bridge, Glen Gairn.

Figure 33: Old Deeside Road, Cairn-na-Quheen, Inver, 1921.

Figure 33A: Old Deeside Road remains near Inver.

From that cairn westwards to Inver a section of the Old Deeside Road runs parallel to the A93 on its south side, but at a lower level. It rises to meet the A93 after about half a mile, just east of Inver. A few remaining derelict buildings sit alongside the old road on this section with the road still traceable on the ground as shown in Figure 33A.

The old road is a little overgrown since the original photo, but the view is still easily recognised. In Fraser's time he notes that the cottages were occupied, but it is no longer the case.

The tent pitched across the old road appears to indicate it was not much used even then. The derelict house in Figure 33A sits below the modern A93 east of Inver. There is an authentic feel of a lost community by the River Dee.

One interesting feature in this spot is the old Inver smiddy or blacksmiths close to the river, now a roofless shell in the trees, as seen in Figure AJ (NO 239 941). It was said to have been powered by a water wheel, reckoned to be the only one directly driven by the River Dee along its whole length. Most water mills used a mill lade to take water from a river to have more control over the flow to the wheel, but this one seems not to have used that method.

Although overgrown, this half mile section of the old road is atmospheric, with the obvious line of the road and buildings clearly seen on the ground. The old road gradually rises, crosses the A93 and can be seen running in front of buildings on the north side of the road. One of them was formerly the post office for Inver. Another, by the A93, is the old toll house of Inver. The Old Deeside Road then crosses the Feardar Burn beside the older disused turnpike road bridge at a ford. The ford has disappeared, although the line of its access can be seen running down by the old mill on the north side of the bridge.

Figure AJ: Old riverside smiddy at Inver.

In the mid 18th century the floating apparition of a severed black hairy hand had terrified the inhabitants of Glen Fearder since the Jacobite rising of 1745. It was known as the spectre of the *Black Han'*. It appeared to the miller one night at the mill and a fierce encounter followed, about which the miller never commented. However, the next morning he dug up the handle of a sword near the mill. According to Fenton Wyness in his book *Royal Valley*, the miller kept the sword hilt hanging above the fireplace, which apparently satisfied the apparition in some way. No further reports of its presence have been reported.

West of Inver, Fraser identifies the excellent walking route along the road on the north side of Meall Alvie as once a commutation road, but not part of the Old Deeside Road between Inver and Invercauld. He concentrates on the section of the A93 through to the Garbh Allt Shiel Bridge. This is the suspension footbridge over the Dee, clearly seen at the side of the A93 east of Invercauld. Fraser identifies this section of the A93 as the Deeside turnpike coinciding with the military road of 1749-53, the Old Deeside Road of 1776 (on Taylor and Skinner's map), and the commutation road prior to 1855.

He then identifies an old road on the slopes to the north of the A93 which would have been the Deeside Road prior to the military road development, putting it into the period before 1750. He traces this from a line which would have come from the former Inver Post Office, behind the Inver Hotel and through fields to pass above Inver Quarry.

The identifiable road then continues the line west to a point where it descends to the A93 near the end of the Inver straight after about half a mile of old road. The best way to find this section of the Deeside Road, which predates the military road, is to walk uphill on a forestry track past Inver Quarry and onto a fairly level terrace running along the hillside just above and parallel to the A93 (NO 223 931). At this point a modern forestry track can be followed west along the terrace.

This probably sits on Fraser's old road because as the modern forestry track starts to climb onto the hill to the right, an old grassy road heads off west and slightly downhill of the rising modern track. This softer old track matches his description as to its place in the landscape. It is remarkable that a section of road from before the middle of the 18th century still exists, making its way through a relatively modern forest plantation. It is shown in Figure AK as a small road, predating the 1750s, west of Inver and running parallel to the modern A93. Obviously when the trees were planted the old road was left clear, now providing an excellent walk above the A93 (NO 213 925).

Figure AK: Old pre 1750s road west of Inver.

Heading west from where this section of very old road joins the A93 the next house along the road is Clagganghoul, which sits on a noticeable bend on the road. Between Clagganghoul and the Garbh Allt Shiel Bridge there is a modern conifer plantation on the north side of the A93 (NO 208 912). Unfortunately it is fenced all round without an obvious access, but gates on the A93 at each end of this section have become dilapidated and entry can be made for the more adventurous follower of the Old Deeside Road.

Just west of Clagganghoul on the north side of the A93, a gate can be entered with the old road gently climbing through the trees to the left of the gate. This rises and opens onto a gap in the plantation for power lines running along the hillside, and then re-enters the trees heading downhill towards the Garbh Allt Shiel Bridge. It remains quite clear to follow until just above the A93, where it stops on a shelf above the road largely invisible from below. It has obviously been truncated by A93 developments over the years.

Again it is remarkable that a modern plantation has preserved about a mile of the old road, although it may yet disappear when the plantation is felled and replanted. Through the plantation the old road has a soft covering of grass, moss and conifer needles, but appears to have a good surface below that. Fraser describes this section as the remains of the older Deeside Road prior to the development of the military road nearer to the Dee. Figure AL shows the Old Deeside Road descending gently west towards the A93 near Clagganghoul (NO 203 911).

Figure AL: Old Deeside Road near Clagganghoul.

Having rejoined the A93 near Garbh Allt Shiel Bridge the old road very quickly turns north off it again just beyond the footbridge on a good estate track (NO 195 909). Again, Fraser reckons this to be the Deeside Road which predates the military road. Figure AM shows the old road heading west towards Keiloch from the Garbh Allt Shiel Bridge.

Figure AM: Old Deeside Road towards Keiloch.

At this point the Old Deeside Road remains on the north side of the Dee and parts company with the old military road for most of the final journey to Braemar. The Old Deeside Road, predating the Invercauld military bridge, now runs along the hillside on the north side of the A93 to the crossroads at Keiloch. Here it intersects the road from the Invercauld bridges to Inver by the north side of Meall Alvie.

Beyond here the Old Deeside Road continues westward as the Invercauld estate road behind Invercauld House and on to Alltdourie. Along this section it has been tarred for a distance and modernised considerably for the estate's use. However, an original part of the Old Deeside Road still remains on the west side of Alltdourie bypassed by the modern track. Figure AN shows this section of old road beside Alltdourie (NO 165 930). It sits on top of a steep bank above the River Dee floodplain.

The old road then goes by a bridge over the Allt an t-Slugain to follow the River Dee to Inverchandlick, a house by the riverside. Inverchandlick means the mouth of the Canlaig, which is the old name of the Slugain Burn.

Figure AN: Old Deeside Road at Alltdourie.

Figure AO: Inverchandlick Cottage by the River Dee.

Figure AP: Old Deeside Road west of Inverchandlick.

At Inverchandlick there was a ford across the Dee which led to Braemar. It was located just below the confluence with the Clunie Water, although there is little sign of it now (NO 150 925). The river has removed traces of the ford over the years, but the location can be seen in Figure AO.

From Inverchandlick the road on the north bank of the Dee continues west as a good estate track, shown in Figure AP (NO 148 926), to Allanaquoich, and onto the tarred minor public road by Mar Lodge and the Linn of Dee. Beyond there it continues to Glen Geldie and Bynack Lodge by old rights of way through the Cairngorm passes. Bynack Lodge and Geldie Lodge are the furthest outposts of habitation on Deeside. Both are now isolated ruins. Bynack was a sheep farm before the Victorian development of the sporting estate at Mar Lodge, while Geldie Lodge was built for deer stalking use.

Chapter 7

The South Deeside Road

Map 9 from Clagganghoul to Braemar covers this area of the old road.

While the foregoing history has related to the North Deeside Road along the Dee valley from Aberdeen, there was a corresponding road on the south side of the Dee, still in use as a public road except for the section through the Balmoral Estate. Fraser includes the section of the South Deeside Road from Invercauld Bridge to the Braemar turnpike toll house where the old north road joins it after crossing the ford at Inverchandlick. The previous chapter described the original North Deeside Road, going from Invercauld by Alltdourie and Inverchandlick to ford the River Dee to reach Braemar. The South Deeside Road described in this chapter is what may be called the original road on the south side of the River Dee to Braemar. Slightly confusingly the modern A93 is usually referred to as the North Deeside Road, even though its last few miles are actually on the south side of the Dee.

Just east of the military bridge at Invercauld a grassy road line leads off the A93 on its south side and heads for the old bridge, while the A93 crosses the Victorian road bridge to the west. This grassy road is the old commutation road which took over the line of the military road of the 1750s. It was replaced by the turnpike and new bridge in the 1850s. It crosses the old Invercauld military bridge and heads to the right in a westerly direction for Braemar. A short section of it still exists as an access to the Balmoral Estate, meeting the A93 coming over the newer bridge. Fraser's Figure 34 is fairly easily replicated. The location can be accessed by a rough path along the riverside from the military bridge. It has really changed very little apart from additional tree growth obscuring part of the old bridge, as can be seen in Figure 34A (NO 185 910).

Figure 34: Old Invercauld Bridge, from the present bridge.

Figure 34A: The view east from the A93 bridge at Invercauld.

Figure 35: Old Invercauld Bridge.

Figure 35A: Old Invercauld Bridge looking west.

Similarly, Fraser's Figure 35 is easily reproduced from a path to the riverside opposite the Keiloch road end on the A93. Again tree growth has extended a little. However, in Fraser's photograph the pier on the left of the main arch appears to be missing the major buttress seen in the modern photograph at Figure 35A (NO 187 909). Presumably it was built to strengthen the bridge sometime in the 20th century.

For about a mile the A93 runs on the line of the military road which was built on top of the old South Deeside Road alongside the River Dee. After this distance a section of old road still exists in the trees on the south side of the A93 which the military road bypassed, and is shown in Figure AQ (NO 174 915). This section coincides with where the Queen's Drive walk comes down to the A93 near the modern council depot. In the trees the old road can still be followed clearly for the most part as a grassy track. The eastern section lies unused while the western end is part of a local path network.

Fraser states that this road predates the military road of the 1750s. Therefore it must be the old South Deeside Road dating back to the 18th century and earlier. As it is higher on the hillside than the A93 it remains out of sight of the passing traffic.

The westerly part of it beyond the council depot now forms part of a local walking route and is easily followed above the A93. The footpath beyond the depot passes a Second World War defensive trench which has been sign-posted along the route.

A final small section of the old south road can just be seen opposite Braemar Castle as a line in a grassy field, but it is disappearing into the land as time passes (NO 156 922). Once past Braemar Castle the A93 meets the old North Deeside Road at the turnpike toll house.

The old North Deeside Road appears as a track coming from the ford at Inverchandlick. Figure AR shows the Braemar toll house on the A93 with the old road to the ford heading off left to the river (NO 153 920).

Figure AQ: Old Deeside Road near the Queen's Drive.

Figure AR: Old toll house at Braemar.

Figure AS: The final section of road into Braemar.

This toll house is interesting because of its style. Turnpike toll houses usually had a semi-circular end projecting onto the road with windows to see oncoming traffic. The Braemar one is in the style of a more conventional cottage, probably because by the time of its construction the heyday of turnpike tolls was waning and subsequently it would be easier to use as a dwelling house. Its original use is still indicated by the windows in the gable walls looking out along the road to monitor road use and collect tolls.

After this point all roads coincide on a straight section rising gradually to enter Braemar, seen in Figure AS (NO 153 920). Fraser notes that when the turnpike was built an embankment was constructed along this section so that coaches could more easily enter Braemar. The original road had a steeper climb which proved awkward for coaches arriving in the village.

Chapter 8

The Braemar Area

Map 9 from Clagganghoul to Braemar covers this area.

Fraser includes several interesting views in the area around Braemar which can still be found. As the military road from Perthshire descends Glen Clunie northwards to Braemar it parts company with the modern A93 and crosses the Clunie on an old military bridge known as Fraser's Bridge, and continues as a single track road into the village. This bridge lies three miles south of Braemar and according to Fraser its military designation was originally the East Bridge, i.e. crossing to the east bank of the Clunie coming from Braemar. The view in Figure 30 is taken from the moorland on the east side of the A93 in Glen Clunie, looking north to Fraser's Bridge. The viewpoint is slightly above the main road on a heathery knoll. The obvious scar on the foreground can still be seen today but it has more heather disguising it in the landscape. Figure 30A shows the present view northward of Fraser's Bridge in Glen Clunie with the A93 in the foreground keeping to the east bank while the military road crossed to the west bank (NO 147 864). It is a fairly timeless scene of the old military road crossing the river in a moorland landscape. In the modern photograph the burnt patches of moorland for grouse management can be readily seen on the far hillside. Fraser also includes his Figure 31, taken from the hillside above Balintuim, on the old military road in Glen Clunie. The golf course occupies the low ground between the military road and the Clunie. Figure 31A shows the present view north towards Braemar from above Balintuim (NO 151 894). For this picture the viewpoint is above the old military road on the west side of the Clunie. The location used for the modern photograph is within a fenced area of new woodland which will eventually obscure the view. Although Fraser mentions the golf course in his photograph, it now appears to have more trees than the earlier picture shows.

Figure 30: Fraser's Bridge, Glen Clunie, 1921.

Figure 30A: Fraser's Bridge, from above the A93.

Figure 31: The old military road to Braemar, Glen Clunie.

Figure 31A: The old military road looking to Braemar.

Figure 37: Present bridge over the River Clunie, Braemar,1905.

Figure 37A: Bridge over the Clunie, Braemar.

Balintuim has an interesting feature associated with it. An original section of the military road runs through the small plantation of trees above the present road. It follows a track on the west side of the buildings, enters the conifer plantation heading south, and after a few hundred yards emerges onto the tarred road again. The present road must have been built alongside the Clunie at a later date, preserving a section of the original road on the hillside above it.

In Braemar he includes photographs of the previous bridge over the Clunie and the newer bridge in his time. He includes the information that the old bridge was regarded as early as 1832 as "very narrow" and was replaced in 1863 by the present one. The newer bridge still spans the river at a scenic rocky section of the river, but has more recent side extensions to allow a widened roadway with pavements. It also must have become too narrow for modern traffic but was modified rather than replaced.

Unfortunately Fraser's Figure 36 cannot be replicated as it is of the earlier demolished Clunie Bridge in Braemar. However, Figure 37 can be approximated from the grassy area behind the Fife Arms Hotel. The open railings on the bridge show where the original parapets have been replaced when it was widened, as can be seen in Figure 37A. This shows the view of the present modified bridge from 1863 over the Clunie seen from the north with the Fife Arms Hotel on the right (NO 151 913).

Chapter 9

Intersection with the Mounth Passes

As mentioned in the introductory chapter, the Mounth is a name used for the range of hills stretching from Aberdeen to Drumochter. The passes which cross it were probably more important in earlier times than the east to west route formed by the Old Deeside Road. At various points the road intersects these older routes which run from north to south, and this section gives a brief summary of these locations. Good information on the old Mounth passes is included in the book *Scottish Hill Tracks*, published by the Scottish Rights of Way and Access Society, 5th Edition of 2011 (ISBN 978-1-907233-16-6). I walked these passes in the years before researching the Old Deeside Road. My photographs are available in the *Mounth Passes Collection* on the Flickr photographic website www.flickr.com/photos/grahamstravels.

Also available via Amazon or Barnes and Noble is an e-book:

The Mounth Passes: A Heritage Guide to the Old Ways Through the Grampian Mountains by Neil Ramsay and Nate Pedersen, with photographs by Graham Marr.

At the start of the Old Deeside Road in Aberdeen it has been noted that the Deeside road diverged from the original main south road, namely the Hardgate. The Hardgate road continued south over the old Bridge of Dee and onwards by the Causey Mounth road to the south. The route went by Banchory Devenick, the causewayed Hare Moss, Muchalls, and on to Cowie, the predecessor of Stonehaven. The remains of the castle at Cowie still sit just to the north of the town.

West of Peterculter the Elsick Mounth follows an old route between Peterculter and Stonehaven crossing the Dee at the ford at Tilbouries just off the old road near the Normandykes Roman Camp. This route linked the lower parts of eastern Aberdeenshire with markets in Kincardine, such as Paldy's Fair at Laurencekirk. The fair was named after St. Palladius, whose ruined chapel is at Auchinblae.

To the east of Crathes lie the old Mills of Drum, now houses, which was the point where the Cryne Corse Mounth crossed the Dee and the Old Deeside Road. This pass linked the old fortified centre at Kincardine on the south of the Mounth with Crathes Castle on Deeside. It is most obviously marked now by passing close to the Durris TV transmitter station which is prominent on the hill. Its continuation north is still called the Couper Road, reflecting the Scots word for the traders who used it.

The Builg and Stock Mounth passes sit close together, linking Glenbervie and Auchinblae on the south of the Mounth with Strachan and Banchory to the north. These were old droving routes for livestock to markets such as Paldy's Fair in the Mearns area. These would have met the road along Deeside at the old centre of Banchory below the cemetery at the east end of the town. A ford through the Dee would have served the Banchory market place.

At Aboyne the Deeside Road intersects the Fungle Road, which fed trade in livestock etc. from Donside and Cromar south to Tarfside in Glen Esk and onwards to Brechin, Forfar and beyond.

A close companion to the Fungle through the same country is the Firmounth Road from Dinnet. It served a similar use linking with the old droving route from Tarland on the east edge of the area of bogs and lochs which was the Muir of Dinnet in former times.

Upper Donside, and beyond that Tomintoul and parts of Speyside, were served by routes such as the Ca Road and Camus Road from Corgarff to Glen Gairn. The Camus Road crosses from Corgarff by Cairn Meadhonach and Tom Odhar to the ruin of Easter Sleach in Glen Gairn. The Ca Road crosses from Corgarff by the east side of the hill named The Ca and heads for

Tullochmacarrick, a ruined farm in Glen Gairn. Glen Gairn itself leads to the Ballater area, and on to the Mounth Keen pass to the south.

Ballater also gives access to Glen Muick, then onwards by the Capel Mounth to Glen Clova and the south. These passes were used by livestock drovers and whisky smugglers, as well as by itinerant harvest workers seeking work in the south.

Crathie, on the Old Deeside Road, was also a crossing point for old passes from Speyside and Glen Gairn. The line of the B976, the old military road, appears to have been a route to Deeside. It is referred to as the Stranyarroch by Amy Stewart Fraser in her book *The Hills of Home*, covering aspects of life in Glen Gairn. From Crathie a route heads south to Glen Muick and then onwards by the Capel Mounth to Glen Clova and Angus.

Braemar itself sits at the hub of several old passes for livestock droving and whisky smuggling. The Bealach Dearg at Invercauld links north to upper Glen Gairn, and onwards, by Loch Builg and Inchrory, to Tomintoul and Speyside. To the south, routes along Glen Clunie take travellers by Glen Callater to the Tolmounth pass into Glen Clova, by Glas Maol to the Monega pass into Glen Isla and by the Cairnwell pass which leads to Glen Shee in Perthshire.

The major Cairngorm passes west of Braemar, namely the Lairig an Laoigh, Lairig Ghru, and Glen Feshie/Glen Geldie, do not directly intersect the Old Deeside Road. However, they link with its western continuation from Inverchandlick through Allanaquoich, Mar Lodge, Linn of Dee and White Bridge to Bynack and Geldie Lodge. The Lairig an Laoigh and Lairig Ghru, emerging onto Deeside near the Linn of Dee could feed trade through Braemar and south by Glen Clunie over the Tolmounth pass, Monega pass or the Cairnwell pass. They also linked to the south through Glen Ey to the Spittal of Glen Shee. The Glen Feshie/Glen Geldie route passed both Geldie and Bynack Lodges, probably going south by Glen Tilt to Blair Atholl. All of these routes eventually fed into the markets of central Scotland.

Figure 38: Part of the remains of Kindrochit Castle, 1908.

Figure 38A: Kindrochit Castle looking to Morrone.

Fraser's Figure 38 is a little difficult to identify, but probably looks north towards Carn na Drochaide across the River Dee. The modern photograph in Figure 38A provides a clearer view looking towards Morrone to the south of the village over the remains of Kindrochit Castle in Braemar, once the controlling point for the passes in the area (NO 151 913).

Conclusion

Revisiting the Old Deeside Road has been an interesting experience. It has taken some investigation to understand Fraser's description and match it to the early 21st century landscape, taking account of housing and road developments along the Dee valley since 1920. From his position, just after the First World War, several factors which now seem long in the past were not that distant to him. It was only around 50-60 years since the tolls on turnpike roads were abolished, within living memory in his day. The building of the turnpike roads themselves had only started about 120-130 years before. He must have thought it worth recording what remained of the old roads before they disappeared from public knowledge.

Looking back the 90 years from today to Fraser's time it is apparent that the Deeside transport systems have changed significantly. At that time the railway connected Aberdeen to Ballater, and the motor powered bus was linking to it from Braemar and other villages along the Dee valley. In the early years of the 20th century my own great grandfather was a carter at Ballater Station, using horse power, and my grandfather drove a traction engine in the Braemar area, helping to build the Victoria Bridge at Mar Lodge. Now the private car, Bluebird bus services, trucks and touring coaches are the main traffic on the A93, and the rail line is largely a walking route, part of the Deeside Way.

However, for those interested in cultural history there are still aspects of Deeside that repay their curiosity. One of these is the discovery that after almost one hundred years, much of the Old Deeside Road still sits in the landscape as Fraser describes it, allowing people to appreciate the old carting route which once serviced the villages along the Dee valley. The original question was whether variations and improvements over the past couple of hundred years have obliterated earlier roads, or were new road lines taken at various times thereby leaving some traces of the older routes as a glimpse into the past. From the investigation carried out for this book it can be seen that there have been losses of some of the features Fraser found. For example, the house at Pittengullies, east of Peterculter, has gone, as has most of the old road in the Ferrar area west of Aboyne, and the section west of Clagganghoul may yet disappear when the plantation is felled, but it is remarkable how much still remains. The objective of this book was to try and identify what might have taken place over the decades by examining the evidence on the ground today. Where possible, this evidence has been documented and supported by the use of the maps, photographs, and written details in this book. Of course, acknowledgement must be paid to G. M. Fraser's original book, which has stood the test of time and is still providing valuable information in the 21st century. The earlier chapter on Maps and Further Information also provides more details of other local books and websites, and these fill out the story of old routes on Deeside.

In summary, the approach taken in this book has been not to simply republish Fraser's findings. I have tried to find on the ground what remains of the old road, to document it, and hopefully to put it into a modern context so that it can be appreciated for what it is. My conclusion is that the Old Deeside Road is an important part of Deeside history. I have found that, despite all the changes since Fraser searched for it, there is still much to see of the old road, some of it modernised and some of it derelict, but all of it reflecting the development of transport and commerce along the Dee valley.

Index of Place Names

Index of Place Names

Index of Place Names

MAPS

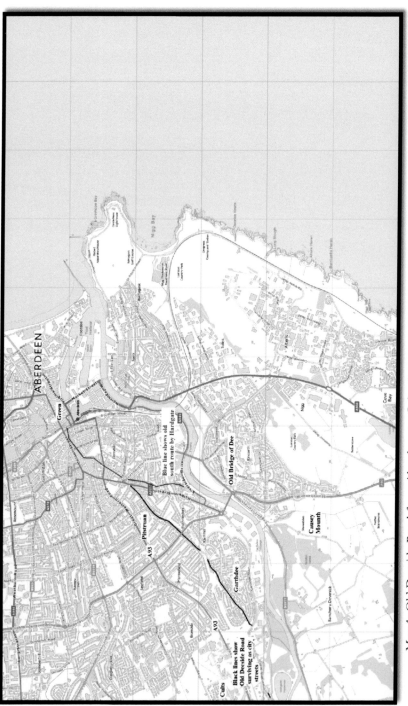

Map 1: Old Deeside Road from Aberdeen to Cults. Contains Ordnance Survey data © Crown copyright and database right (2014)

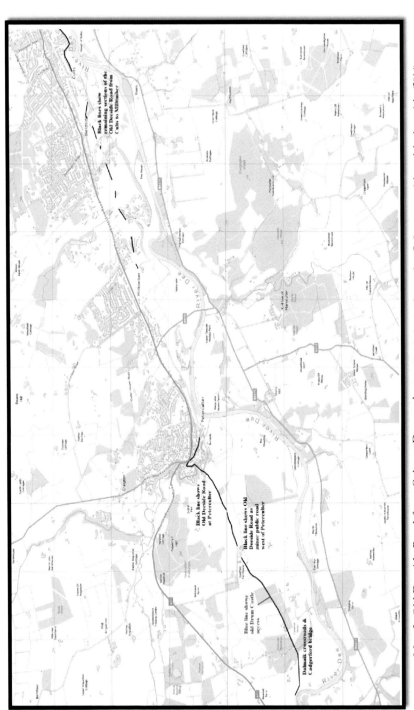

Map 2: Old Deeside Road from Cults to Drumoak. Contains Ordnance Survey data © Crown copyright and database right (2014)

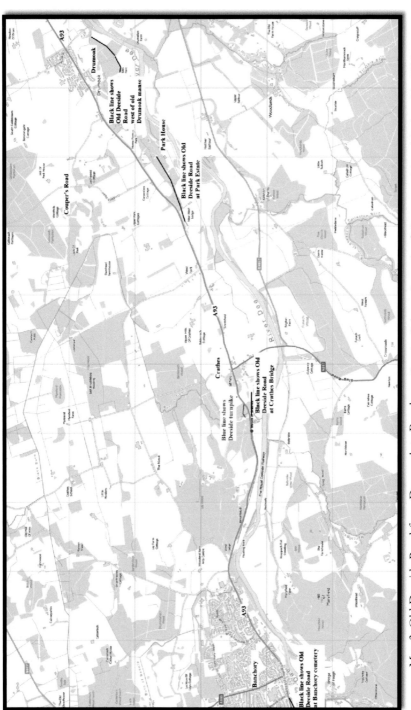

Map 3: Old Deeside Road from Drumoak to Banchory. Contains Ordnance Survey data © Crown copyright and database right (2014)

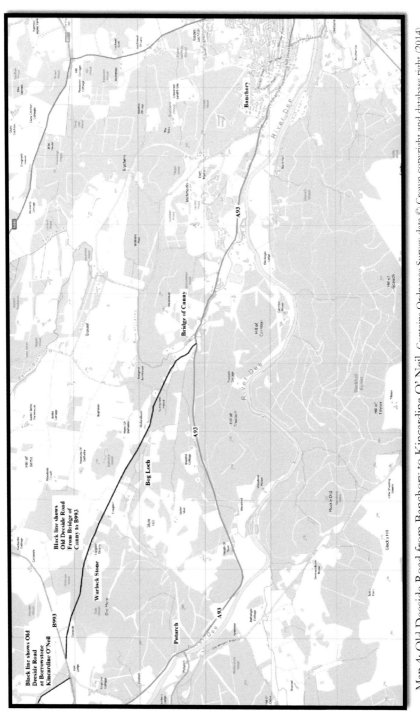

Map 4: Old Deeside Road from Banchory to Kincardine O' Neil. Contains Ordnance Survey data © Crown copyright and database right (2014)

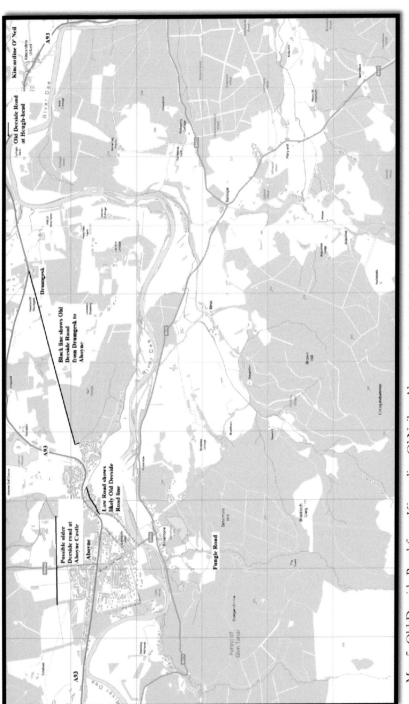

Map 5: Old Deeside Road from Kincardine O' Neil to Aboyne. Contains Ordnance Survey data © Crown copyright and database right (2014)

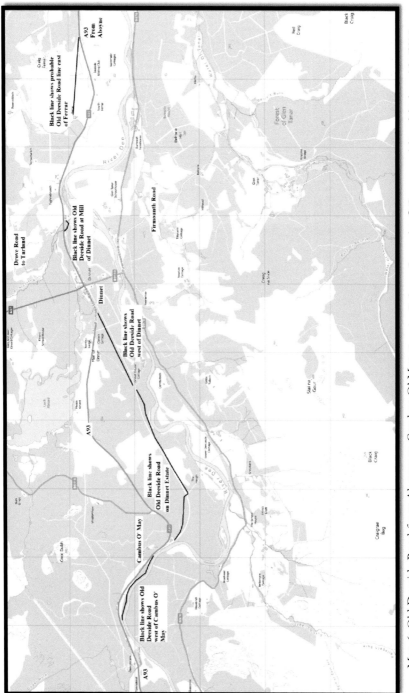

Map 6: Old Deeside Road from Aboyne to Cambus O' May. Contains Ordnance Survey data © Crown copyright and database right (2014)

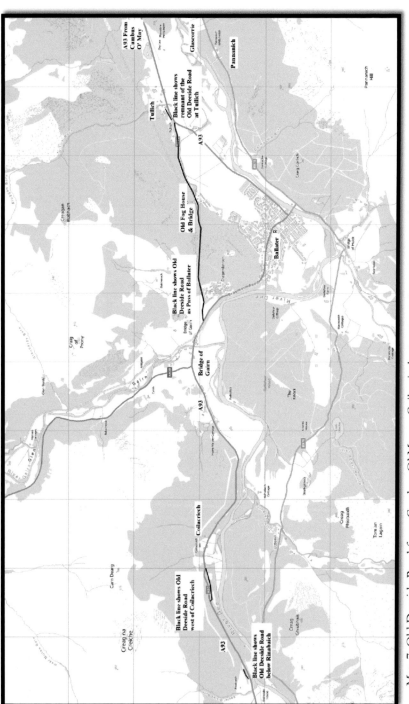

Map 7: Old Deeside Road from Cambus O' May to Coilacriech. Contains Ordinance Survey data © Crown copyright and database right (2014)

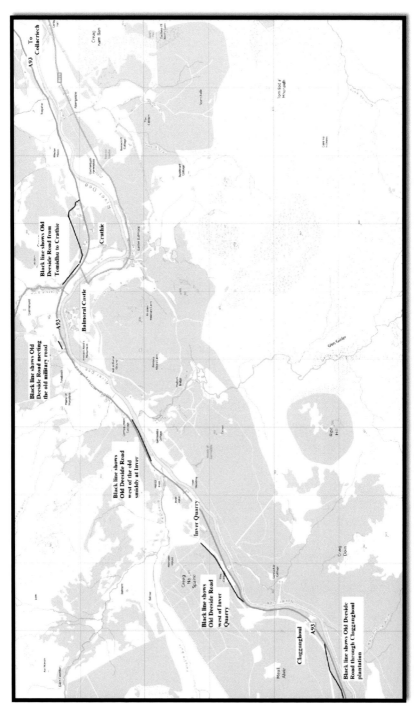

Map 8: Old Deeside Road from Coilacriech to Clagganghoul. Contains Ordnance Survey data © Crown copyright and database right (2014)

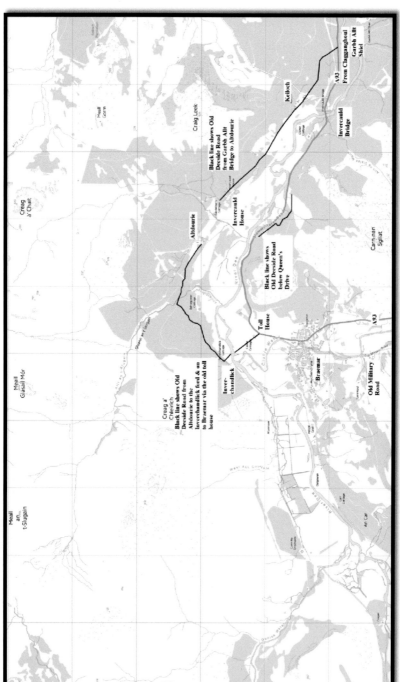

Map 9: Old Deeside Road from Clagganghoul to Braemar. Contains Ordnance Survey data © Crown copyright and database right (2014)